SRI LANKA CALLING

A Spiritual Journey

DR KERSTIN JOOST

Sri Lanka Calling

The information given in this book should not be treated as a substitute for professional medical advise. Always consult a medical practitioner.

Although the author and publisher have made every effort to ensure that the information in this book was correct at press time, the author and publisher do not assume and hereby disclaim any liability to any party for any loss, damage, or disruption caused by errors or omissions, whether such errors or omissions result from negligence, accident, or any other cause.

This is a work of non-fiction and parts of this book has been fictionalised for purpose of a narrative.

Copyright © Kerstin Joost 2020

All rights reserved. No part of this book may be reproduced in any form without permission in writing from the publisher, except by a reviewer who may quote brief pages in review.

1st Edition, November 2020

Book Design by www.bodhi-design.co.uk

ISBN 978-1-913479-66-4 (paperback)

ISBN 978-1-913479-67-1 (ebook)

Published by That Guy's House

www.ThatGuysHouse.com

A FEW WORDS ABOUT THE NEW EDITION

Since the publication of my book at the beginning of 2017, a lot has happened - an enormous amount. My experiences in Sri Lanka, writing about them, and also the reactions of my readers have triggered deep processes within me. I have reflected on my feelings and my actions, and today I see everything not only from a temporal distance, but also from a different perspective. With more understanding, more compassion, more acceptance. This feels very good, very peaceful. I am now even proud of what I have experienced and will share it all with you in this book, without any embellishments. It has been a long journey to get where I am today. I could have gone another way, but I always knew that the choices were mine to make. I could be full of anger and disappointment now, but I am not. I have grown from my experiences and I owe this to many great qualities I came to recognise in myself: my courage, the ability to stand up again and again, my patience, and finally, my strong desire to make the best of my experiences.

We all see our experiences from a very small perspective. We are humans, not birds and not angels. At the time of the third edition of my book (2020), exactly ten years have passed since I embarked on the greatest adventure of my life so far. I now see everything with new eyes, from a fresh perspective. I have discovered the spiritual dimension of my experiences and this has given me a deep inner peace - and a sense of pride now fills me. I see things differently today, because I set out on a quest and wanted to understand why all of this happened to me. And, fortunately, I met people who helped me find answers. People who were able to make sense out of my horoscope and numerology. It took patience until these insights came together, but I didn't want to give up. It was all worth it, and today I am happy to share my experiences as well as my new perspective with you. I remember how excited I was when I first saw my book on Amazon. I was proud, yet at the same time still very ashamed. However, an inner voice guided me and gave me the confidence that sharing my story was necessary and important. And that voice spoke the truth! I never expected that writing would help me heal so much. But even less had I expected to inspire so many people, especially women, with my writing! So, with this edition, I am taking a big step forward and finally publishing my experiences under my real name. Three years ago, I needed a pseudonym to hide behind. Today I can fully stand by my story and I am ready to show myself. With this book, I want to show you that what we experience is not the most important thing: it is about how we deal with those experiences. But this will become clear at the end of the story. For now, I invite you on a journey to a tropical country in the Indian Ocean. Join me on the courageous journey to follow the voice of the heart!

This book is an adventure story in which I share true experiences with you. Only the names of the players and places have been changed. I am as open as possible so that you, the reader, can understand the path that led me, step by step, to these experiences. I followed my heart, but it felt like I had forgotten my mind; I saw it this way for a long time. But today, more than ever, it feels as if there was no other way for me. As if that's the way it was meant to be. My book is about my great love for the people of Sri Lanka and for the country where the light brings forth such particularly intense colours. I love colours and I still love this island, despite everything. After sharing my backstory, I will tell you everything about my time in Sri Lanka. Finally, I will share the treasures I found after my return: knowledge, acceptance, and inner ways of processing and healing. And you will learn how I became the self-confident woman I am today. How I discovered in myself a lot of courage, patience, endurance, energy, compassion, and love. And the ability to forgive. For this, the experiences on my dream island were essential, and for this, I am grateful today. I now wish you much pleasure in reading.

– Kerstin Joost

Contents

Invitation	9
Goodbye Hamburg	13
My Own Practice	21
Sri Lanka Calls	25
First Impressions	29
Ayurveda is Great	35
New Attempt	43
It Can't Go On Like This	47
Where is Your Husband?	51
Surprise	57
Home - Where is That?	61
New Year Greetings and an Invitation	67
Welcome to Sri Lanka	75
He's Waiting Under a Palm Tree	81
Love Love Love	89
A Great Idea	93
The Adventure Begins	97
Shopping	105
Variety	111
Meetings and Musings	117

There Will Be a Wedding	127
A Step Into the Unknown and How an Angel Catches Me	133
Welcome Back	141
I Celebrate Myself	145
The Next Chapter	153
Plan A or Plan B	157
My Life as a Teacher in Sri Lanka	161
The Villa	171
Let Go	181
Love Heals	187
Time to Go Back	201
And How Do I Live Now?	205
From a Distance, Everything Looks Different - What the Stars Say	211
Colours Give Me Insights into Past Lives	215
My Outer Journey was an Inner Journey	221
My Offerings	225

Sri Lanka Calling

CHAPTER 1:

Invitation

The desire to travel must have always been within me. I remember my first favourite record, but I have no idea how it got into my hands after I got my first record player at the age of twelve. This record player was my first way of listening to music, long before the time of CDs and downloads. The turntable was mounted on a huge radio, one of those with braided covers in front of the speakers and mechanical buttons to switch from radio to record. There were huge beige knobs for changing volume and stations. I loved this monster. My parents could finally afford a real stereo system of their own, and they had bequeathed me this antique. With it came my first records: the Beatles Blue Album and a fairy tale record, called The Journeys of Ulysses. This became my favourite album. On the cover was a giant with an eye on his forehead - a cyclops, I learned - and frightened little men were running around him. These were Ulysses and his men. I listened to the tale, my heart racing as I heard how the giant threw boulders at the men, and to save themselves and get back to their ship, they hid among a flock of sheep. These stories fascinated me. I loved this record and listened to it over and over again, although it is not light-hearted fare. On his journeys, Ulysses had to fight for his life again and again, and I was awed by the exploits of this brave adventurer. He met one danger after another and many of his companions died along the way. Only Ulysses survived in the end and returned to Ithaca, where his wife and son were waiting for him, after an absence of many years. He was home at last. What did he bring back from his travels? Gold, jewels, possessions? None of the above. He brought back experiences, had grown and matured in his challenges. Ulysses had not only come home physically, but also emotionally. It had been a spiritual journey, a rite of initiation. But I only realised this much later - when I came home from my own journey.

I think about this story again and again and find it interesting that I was obsessed with it so early in life. Because I too have been travelling all my life. And, like Ulysses, I experienced many adventures that pushed me to my limits, that challenged me, at times against my will. Because my adventures were never things like bungee jumping or free-climbing – extreme activities others consciously choose to do for fun or to overcome their fears. It seems instead as if life has always presented me with challenges to overcome and tasks to face – and they were rarely enjoyable! They always confronted me with the question of what I should give preference to: my mind or my feelings. Heart over head or head over heart? Sri Lanka and its people played an important role on my path and I can honestly say that I spent the most beautiful moments of my life there. But also the most difficult ones. The country and its people have called me, challenged me, loved me, worshipped me, hurt me, but also healed me. Without these experiences, I would not be the woman I am today. These encounters played a formative role in my search for my home. They helped me to find my true home - in myself. I only now know what is important and right for me and I set my priorities differently than before. Now I am the number one in my life. I have learned that a healthy sense of self-love is the basis for a fulfilled life and also for healthy relationships with other people. Today, I live free and independent yet still feel connected to everything that exists. Therefore, I thank all who I met on my journeys and who are now part of my life. Every life path is different, and not every person has to face the same challenges. I hope from the bottom of my heart that yours are easier! But now, I invite you to dive into my travel memoirs with me and listen to Sri Lanka's call.

Sri Lanka Calling

CHAPTER 2:

Goodbye Hamburg

It was in 1997, over twenty years ago, when Sri Lanka first came into my consciousness. It appeared out of nowhere, like a whale surfacing from the vastness of the sea. Yet it felt as if it had always been with me, in my heart. And it attracted me magnetically, or rather magically. The land seemed to cry out to me: Come home, Kerstin! If you keep hearing such a strong call, you just have to go, don't you? I could hardly put wax in my ears, like Ulysses did to protect himself from the call of the sirens. The call came from inside. At the time of this call, I was living in Switzerland with my husband, Walter. I was born and raised in Germany, but I have always been a wanderer. Perhaps I get this from my parents, who also had to search for a new home, seeking a better life. My parents are from East Germany, but they emigrated to the West in 1961, knowing they had a limited amount of time to leave the country before the Wall went up between East and West Germany. Via Berlin, they were among the last who were able to travel to the western part of the city before the closing of the Wall, and then were flown out to Hamburg. They left their homeland and also their families behind without knowing if and when they would see them again. And without really knowing what awaited them on the other side. My parents were brave, especially because my mother was six months pregnant with me. On top of that, neither of them had any vocational training: my father studied mechanical engineering and was in his last semester, and my mother was in the middle of studying medicine. They left anyway and were convinced that they could make a new start. They wanted to give their child a greater freedom than they had ever experienced before. It was not an easy start in the West: my father had to start his studies all over again because his certifications were not recognised at the new universities. My mother was allowed to continue her studies, because different rules applied to her course. I was born in the summer of 1961 in Hamburg. We did not stay there for long. For various reasons, which had to do with my parents' courses of study and a part-time job for my father, the three of us moved to Aachen shortly after my birth and stayed there for six years. I went to school in this city, and my three siblings were born; I don't know much more from that time. When I was almost seven, we moved to a small town in Schleswig-Holstein, a state in Northern Germany, where I went to school for four years. Then we moved on to a village between Hamburg and Segeberg, from where I had a long bus ride to the city of the Karl May Festival. I was not alone, however: I sat together with three school friends on the trip and played card games. Nice snapshots in my memory. After another two years we moved to another small town, even closer to Hamburg. There I graduated from high school with excellent grades, which I still think is rather impressive after the many school changes. Biology and mathematics were my major subjects, a choice that would be different if I had to choose again today. But art was also part of my studies – that choice still fits today. I only returned to my hometown for my own medical studies and spent the entire six years there until I got my license to practice medicine.

My childhood was marked by constantly changing caregivers and many farewells. I learned through my experiences that it was not worthwhile to make new friends, because I would soon lose them again anyway. I was always quiet, with much going on beneath the surface, like a deep lake, as I once wrote in my poetry journal. I did not talk much and withdrew more and more into my shell. There was also a lot of tension at home: my parents were under enormous pressure to feed us all. They had no state support in the West and no help with childcare, because all the grandmothers and aunts who could normally help look after the children were far away. There was a growing crisis between the two of them and I, as the oldest, tried to mediate. My parents did not speak much to each other and the air was thick with their unspoken words. I was a highly sensitive child, noticed everything and tried to avoid thunderstorms. So, I was as quiet as possible and took care of my little sisters. Early on, I learned to anticipate the needs of others and to put them before my own. It took me decades to get used to looking after my own needs again.

I had my own apartment in Hamburg while I was studying medicine. I liked the Gateway to the World, as Hamburg is known, with its big harbour and ships full of people traveling all round the world; I loved the Alster and Elbe rivers, the waterways and bridges, and the many parks. They say Hamburg has more bridges than Venice, and I love bridges. They connect. I also always wanted to be a bridge between my parents, but it was exhausting. After the state exams, I couldn't find a job in my hometown and had to move. I had felt a strong connection to the English language for a long time and felt the desire to live in England for a while. An employment contract with a hospital was already on my desk, but at the last moment I changed my plans: a man came along and changed everything. I had done an internship in Switzerland during the last year of my studies and there, during a holiday on Lake Como, I met Walter. We were both in the same surf school and while I was standing for the first (and only) time on a surfboard, Walter was there with some friends. We stayed in touch and our relationship deepened through mutual visits, until I finally moved to Switzerland with him in 1989. The contents of my student dormitory were sold quickly, and I was able to send six moving boxes by train to Zurich. This was the start of a new phase in my life and my first international move. A few more were to follow.

Walter was a very cosy person: rather strong build, not overly muscular, but very cuddly. Very nice and soft to snuggle up with! He could easily enjoy an evening at home with a glass of red wine, a fine meal, and me. I liked that. We talked a lot, philosophised about life and made ourselves comfortable together. Walter liked taking pictures, playing the classical guitar, and being out in nature: he liked to go hiking, cross-country skiing or cycling. As he had been a scout for many years, he loved everything that had to do with making fire and woodwork. He was twenty-four when we met (I was twenty-seven) and he took our relationship slowly - comfortably. I liked that a lot about him, because I was a restless woman who longed for stability. Wild and changeable like my star sign, Gemini, the twins. I had been in a few relationships, but at that time I had been single for two years. Walter lived near Zurich, and while he was working, I sent applications from his apartment to the whole of German-speaking Switzerland. I first received a few rejections, until I was finally invited for an interview in the canton of Obwalden. (A canton is similar to a district or state, with its own local government; there are twenty-six cantons in total in Switzerland.) 'Sarnen? Where is that?' asked Walter, who had never been to the canton in between the mountains before. 'Typically Zurich,' people from Central Switzerland would now say about this lack of knowledge of anything outside the city, much like how Londoners think no life exists beyond the M25. While Zurich is full of people who love the city lifestyle, Sarnen is rural, surrounded by mountains, full of farmers, cows, yodelling – quintessential Switzerland. It was here that I felt for the first time that worlds lay between the two cantons, even though you can cover the distance in an hour by car. The people of Zurich are known for their pride in staying close to their beloved city. Now that I have a Swiss passport and live in the canton of Zurich, I can understand that very well. But more about that later!

Walter got to know Central Switzerland along with me, because I got the job at the local hospital. He worked in Zurich and attended night school after work, which was very strenuous and time-consuming. At the beginning, we only saw each other on weekends and slowly got to know each other better. After this first job, I had a few more in hospitals in the area and then lived in furnished holiday apartments, often on farms. The walls were panelled with wood, the ceilings were low, and the curtains were red-and-white checked, just like in the tourist brochures or in the film Heidi. I always felt like I was on holiday there. I loved Swiss specialities like raclette and cheese fondue, as well as the Swiss dialect, and the beautiful landscape of mountains and lakes. After Walter finished his apprenticeship, we quit our jobs and took some time off. For nine months we travelled the world; we cycled through Norway and California, through Baja California (Mexico) and New Zealand. It was a kind of trial run for our future life together and we liked it very much. It was fun to just live into the day, in the moment, and discover new things again and again. I also enjoyed being in nature around the clock; we had a tent with us and used it as often as we could. Never was I physically as fit as I was at that time. During the trip, we decided to get married after our return and started to plan our wedding. To be honest, that was after I had asked Walter. We had already overcome some difficulties together and I thought we were a good match. So, I asked him the question of all questions. Looking back, I guess it was my big wish to find an anchor in marriage. To have a person who was there for me, as well as a common apartment, a home as well as someone to come home to. Walter was able to offer me all of this. The matter was decided, and Walter and I got married half a year after our return to Switzerland, in the canton of Obwalden, on the beautiful Lake Sarnen.

We then rented our first apartment together in the neighbouring canton of Nidwalden, another rural area with mountains and lakes and many brown cows. It was really just like living in a picture book! Walter found a job there in financial controlling, and we furnished our first apartment together. My family loved to visit us, because we always took them on such nice trips into the mountains - and fed them cheese fondue. I gained experience in various fields of orthodox medicine and finally specialised in general medicine. But orthodox medicine satisfied me less and less. I wanted to get to the bottom of the diseases instead of merely curing symptoms, and was looking for a deeper healing method. After a bit of soul searching, I finally decided to go for homeopathy. In 1995, I started an intensive two-year training program at a homeopathy school in Zug. In order to finance this, I gave lessons in basic medical subjects such as anatomy and physiology at the same school, so I was fully occupied six days a week. It was a very intense time, actually much too much for me. But I persevered, and eventually graduated as a homeopath. This shows you that I am a fighter, something that would help me greatly in many more experiences to come. After Walter and I had been married for two years and I had already lived in Switzerland for five years, I was able to get naturalised and got a Swiss passport. Unfortunately, I had to give up my German passport for this, which I did not like at all. I was and still am German! But since German law did not allow dual citizenship at that time and I no longer felt like walking around with a foreigner's identity card, I took the opportunity to become naturalised. Fortunately, I did not have to pass an exam to do so, but my students at the homeopathy school did a test with me for fun, just like in The Swissmakers. This is a film with Emil Steinberger, in which the Swiss naturalisation practice is taken for a ride. A very funny film! In my test, I only had to say a few words in Swiss German and name a few cantons. We had a lot of fun and I was touched that they'd made the effort. Of course, I passed with flying colours and we celebrated the occasion! I was naturalised in Regensdorf, a small town in the canton of Zurich, and since then I've had a certificate of origin and a Swiss hometown. Regensdorf is Walter's birthplace, so I became a citizen of Regensdorf and thus a citizen of the canton of Zurich. So now I had a home. Everything was good.

Sri Lanka Calling

CHAPTER 3:

My Own Practice

After I got my diploma as a homeopath in 1997, I was delighted to open my own practice: Dr. Kerstin Joost, Practice for Classical Homeopathy. I was very proud of myself. I still remember our euphoria: looking for suitable rooms, choosing furniture and pictures. There was a small table and chairs for children with lots of toys and a very popular wooden cooking stove. My little patients always made me feel wonderful, and prepared many imaginary meals for me at this little stove. And I even had a terrace with lots of sun for my breaks, because the practice was on the ground floor. It was the fulfilment of my dreams and I was very, very happy. I placed a small advertisement in the local newspaper, and Walter and I quickly went on holiday for a few days. That was the calm before a big storm! When I checked the answering machine, I couldn't believe my ears: the tape was full! Countless people had called to make appointments with me. A tsunami of expectations was rolling in on me as I listened to their messages. My heart was beating with joy, excitement, and of course fear of this new challenge. Would I be able to do all this? My husband had written a simple computer program for me and I planned to do all the billing with the health insurance companies myself. He wanted to do the bookkeeping. I bought myself a chest of drawers where I kept my homeopathic medicines. Countless tiny glass bottles were stored there so that I could give any remedy to my patients. An examination couch, my desk and a stethoscope - that was all I needed. I opened the doors to my first own practice and was happy to finally apply what I had learned in the two years at homeopathy school. Finally, I would be able to help people to heal their illnesses in a gentle yet profound way. My patients liked me and my open-minded, cheerful manner. They had confidence in me, since I brought along orthodox medical experience - even though I no longer applied it. And there was something else that contributed to the rapid success of my practice at that time: homeopathy was in fashion. It was like a new wave of opening, acceptance, trust in this healing method, which was not so new. At the beginning of the 19th century, Samuel Hahnemann had formulated its basic laws and tested the remedies I was now working with. In some countries, this healing method has been established much longer than in Germany; in England there are even homeopathic clinics. And it is said that even the royal family is enthusiastic about it. However, in Germany, it's still debated whether or not homeopathy is a legitimately effective medical practice. Anyway, for many good reasons, people seeking help now flocked to my practice with their children; apparently, I was in the right place at the right time. I was mighty proud to reside behind my big desk and prescribe my remedies. The desk was really huge, I think nearly two meters long, and beautiful. I was completely absorbed in this work and some years later, after I had to say goodbye to my practice, I even got the opportunity to write a doctoral thesis in the field of homeopathy. My topic was 'Patient Satisfaction in Comparison: Conventional Medicine and Homeopathy'. For this, many patients had been asked which form of therapy they preferred. I was not surprised that homeopathy was ahead in this field.

CHAPTER 4:

Sri Lanka Calls

Sadly, it didn't take long until I wasn't quite so happy. I think it was just a few months. I had trouble switching off: I thought about my clients in the evening too, I did emergency service on weekends, felt the responsibility keenly. I burned out. I no longer enjoyed the many new patients, squeezing my brain for the right medication and looking for solutions. One day it was clear to me: I urgently needed to go on holiday, and I needed to go alone! I can't explain it to this day, but I still see myself determined and clear, saying to Walter 'I know what I need: I'm doing an Ayurveda retreat in Sri Lanka!' I have no idea where this idea came from. In 1997, Sri Lanka was not exactly on the hit list of Booking.com or Tripadvisor, because the north of the island was a war zone and one was never sure if bombs would go off at the international airport in Colombo. In 2001 there was actually an airplane attack by the Tamil Tigers on the airport; a civil war had already been going on for eighteen years at that point. Strangely enough, I also knew with great certainty that I wanted to do Ayurveda. How did I come up with that? There might have been something about it in the women's magazines at the time, but I was and am still not a reader of beauty and health magazines. Who or what inspired me, I cannot say. But I am quite sure that such decisions, those which are important for our lives, are guided by higher forces that have the big picture in mind. Because seen from a distance, even things you don't understand at first glance - like this decision - make sense. There would be many more such inspirations in my life, and I followed this first one without hesitation.

Fortunately, I quickly found a fill-in for my practice, which I naturally did not want to neglect. Next, I needed a visa. This was not as easy as today: I had to send my passport to the Sri Lankan Consulate in Bern. But to apply for the visa, I needed a hotel address first. Where did I want to go anyway? I got some catalogues from the travel agency and searched the internet. A hotel immediately jumped at me: the Hotel Svedana, at the southern tip of Sri Lanka. It was praised as one of the oldest and biggest hotels on the island and I found only positive comments. It was said to offer real, traditional Ayurveda and was exclusively for guests who wanted to do an intensive detoxification program. One should plan two, or even better, three weeks for such a course. I liked the description and the photos of the Hotel Svedana at first sight and I booked a stay of fourteen days. Great, now I could apply for the visa and go shopping! I bought some light summer clothes, as the travel guides said that it was expected to be around 30 degrees all year round. It was just spring in our country, so luckily, there were already light cotton things in the shops. And I opened my first e-mail account; I still remember it well. Unbelievable, but I had lived quite well without emails until then! Today, I can't imagine a life without emails and social media anymore – incredible, how fast it changed. Finally, all preparations were done and we could start: off to the retreat! Two weeks in a country I didn't know. Which was very far away. To a treatment I had almost no idea about. Alone. But I was quite sure that it was the right thing for me. Walter took me to the airport in Zurich and we said goodbye, full of hope that I would feel better when I got back. I travelled with Sri Lankan Airlines, which at that time still flew directly from Zurich. I was incredibly excited when I boarded the plane! Walter and I had travelled a lot together, but this trip was all mine. I was not afraid, because I knew that I would be picked up at the airport in Colombo by a driver from the hotel. And at the hotel I had a complete carefree package. So, I was able to relax right from the start and was happy to be free of the burden of my responsibilities.

CHAPTER 5:

First Impressions

I remember exactly in which month I arrived in Sri Lanka for the first time: it was definitely in April, towards the end. Why do I remember it? The drive from the airport to the hotel was forever etched in my memory. I was picked up at the airport in Colombo, as previously agreed. In the arrival hall, there was a driver with my name on a placard and we found each other quickly. I was his only passenger that early morning. It was just getting light when I got into the white minibus and finally, I could stretch out a bit. The airport of the capital is located on the west coast, about halfway along the island. It is only approximately 130 kilometres to the Hotel Svedana at the southern tip, but at that time, there was no other way than to drive on the bumpy coastal road through many small villages. Today, there is the Expressway - the only motorway on the island - that connects the airport and Matara at the south. An enormous advantage for the many hotels at the west and south coasts. Also, since then a second airport has been built in the south-east of the island, a complete complex with congress centre and international harbour - the legacy of a former president – which is hardly used. But back then we took the scenic route through endless Colombo and finally through the awakening villages. I saw people sleeping in front of closed shops, many poor wooden huts but also many stone houses and shops with large modern shop windows. Cows slowly started their search for food and crossed the road comfortably, emaciated dogs searched in packs for something edible. The first people stood at the roadside with freshly oiled hair, waiting for the bus. Many women wore colourful saris, a beautiful sight. My driver didn't speak much; on the radio, there was soft Sri Lankan music playing. I let the many new impressions pass by me and enjoyed the anticipation of staying in a beautiful hotel. Although I would have loved to sleep, I wanted to take in everything, and it was worth it: suddenly the row of houses ended on the right side of the street and we drove directly along the beach! An unobstructed view of the Indian Ocean, white sand, waves, fishing boats ... my heart was laughing! Yes, here is where I was meant to be, here I could relax. I was dog-tired from the long journey and happy that from now on I did not have to worry about anything. Or did I have to? I suddenly noticed that my driver was driving slower and slower and our vehicle was drifting more and more to the right. In Sri Lanka there is left-hand traffic, so the right side was oncoming traffic – so this drifting was not good at all, as a car could come towards us at any time. He seemed to be more tired than me, because at some point I realised that he kept dozing off again and again. My goodness! I had to wake him up and said we'd better take a break. He agreed and we stopped at the side of the road. There we stood for a while in the fresh sea air and stretched our tired limbs. It takes about five hours to cover this distance and I know by now that the drivers can only sleep briefly in their bus after they have already completed the five (or more, depending on the traffic) hours for the way there. But what had completely killed this man were the many parties he had experienced in the past days. This is another reason I know it must have been April, because this is the party month par excellence in Sri Lanka. A time full of celebrations, which result from the lunar calendar. In April, both the Sinhalese and the Tamils celebrate their New Year festivities and these last for several days. Sri Lanka is a country where people of different religions and ancestries live. The majority are Buddhists, but there are also many Muslims and Christians and (fewer) Hindus, who today live together in a predominantly peaceful and tolerant way. Since the Buddhists are numerically dominant, their temples can be found in every village. White stupas, prayer flags, and orange-robed monks belong to Sri Lanka and can be found on every postcard. With greetings from Sri Lanka! Every full moon day is a national holiday, called Poja Day, when schools, banks, and authorities are closed. Some of these Poja Days are particularly important and are celebrated for a correspondingly long time (over several days). On the full moon between the end of April and middle of May, the most important religious and cultural festival, Vesak, takes place. On this day, the birth, enlightenment, and entering into nirvana of Buddha are celebrated simultaneously. This joyous festival has been happening every year for more than 1,000 years! In 1999, the UN recognized Vesak Day to acknowledge the contribution that Buddhism, one of the oldest religions in the world, has made for over 2,500 years. This day is commemorated annually at the UN Headquarters and other UN offices and missions. So, as you can imagine, April in Sri Lanka is full of parties, and sleep is often missed out. Later, I was able to participate in some of these celebrations and I will tell you more about them later. Suffice it to say, alcohol plays an important role in these celebrations. And I think my driver had consumed a lot of it, but had not had much sleep. After he had inhaled his life-saving cigarettes on the beach and I had inhaled the fresh sea air, we drove on without further crises.

After what felt like an eternity, we reached our destination, awake and safe. The Hotel Svedana forms a big hotel complex right at the sea. It is separated from the street by a high wall, and at first sight it does not appear to be very inviting. When we arrived, my driver honked and a man in light brown uniform stepped out of the guard house. After an exchange of words, we were allowed to pass and the big gate opened, squeaking. In front of the spacious entrance of the hotel, I got out of the air-conditioned minibus and got my first taste of the air of the tropics: it was warm, humid, heavy, and smelled like flowers. I started sweating immediately. I was travelling in jeans and trainers – it had been quite cold in Switzerland after all. But this attire was much too warm for the heat of Sri Lanka! I wanted to throw everything off me and jump into the sea. But that had to wait, because now I was warmly welcomed: a German hostess appeared and handed me a cool, damp towel, which was wonderfully scented with jasmine. I rubbed my face and neck with it and cooled my overheated forearms and hands. Divine! Then she handed me an opened yellow coconut with a straw so that I could drink the delicious watery juice. 'This is a King Coconut,' she explained, 'which grows everywhere in Sri Lanka. You can also buy it at the roadside when you are travelling and thus have a cheap, refreshing and hygienically perfect drink: the nuts are only opened with a knife after purchase.' I experienced all these impressions as if through cotton wool: I was so infinitely tired, my feet swollen from sitting, cramped and hot in my winter clothes. While I slurped from my coconut, I still had time for a first impression of the hotel. The hostess sat down with me and her words came to me through the fog of tiredness. She explained to me that this house had been built especially for Ayurveda treatments and that there was no air conditioning in the common rooms. The spa guests should stay in a warm climate around the clock so that the treatments were more intensive. Therefore, the construction of the complex was very airy and there was no entrance door. The ground floor was a wide-open hall – therefore, the wall separating it from the street was needed. So, from my chair in the hall I could look directly at the sea without being separated from it by glass. It was exquisitely beautiful! I knew I had chosen the right hotel. To be near the sea, in the warmth of the tropics, was half the medicine for me. Finally, my coconut was empty, and I was led to the first floor by a porter. My suitcase was already waiting in my room. And a delightful surprise: I had a room with a sea view! The gauzy curtains were blowing in the wind and through the open balcony door I could hear the surf. A big bed with starched white sheets welcomed me, decorated with hibiscus flowers. A large framed mirror, a table and chair, and a cupboard completed the furnishings. Next door was my spacious bathroom, pure luxury. And in addition to all of this, two whole weeks of time – how wonderful! I quickly took off my warm clothes and fell onto the four-poster bed – I just wanted to stretch out and lie down, not thinking about anything anymore, and just let go. I had arrived, in the land of my dreams, in a wonderful, healing place. It dawned on me, listening to the waves and letting myself fall into this delicious feeling, that all was well.

CHAPTER 6:

Ayurveda is Great

I experienced valuable and nourishing days in this Ayurveda hotel. On the second day, I had my first doctor's appointment. The doctor spoke English with a delightful Asian accent. I love the combination of the Asian accent with the English accent. The up and down of the words is like a dance, a chanting. And the head wagging, wonderful. The German hostess did not have much to translate for me, but she noted down all the instructions of the doctor. He asked me about my past illnesses and my current complaints. Then he placed three fingers on my wrist to check my pulse, from which he could read the causes of my exhaustion. That must be great, I thought, if you can find out so much about a person with such a simple examination. Later I learned how complex this art of healing is and that doctors need years to correctly assess one pulse. In Ayurveda, it is assumed that all diseases are caused by an imbalance of the five elements. These are fire, water, earth, air, and space. Our body, every single part, is made up of these building blocks, they say. It is subject to many influences through our diet, life habits, and also the seasons, moon phases, and much more. If you are familiar with these connections, you can actively do something to get healthy or – better – not get sick in the first place. Later, I noticed that the Sri Lankans have really internalised this knowledge. They still know which plants warm the body when they have a cold during the monsoon season, or which cool the body when it is hot. We in the West have forgotten much of the knowledge of our ancestors. Surely this is related to the fact that healers in the West had been persecuted and killed as witches for centuries if they worked with natural remedies. That persecution did not exist in the East. I learned a lot about these connections in the course of my cure, because in the evenings the doctors gave a lecture in which they explained all of this to us.

But back to my treatment. The doctor determined which elements were mixed up in my case. He found a Vata disorder, which means I had too much air in my body, and also in my mind. The cause was too much brooding, too much mental work. I believed this immediately; I had really experienced a lot of this. First, the training as a homeopath, while at the same time working as a teacher, then my practice with many doubts about whether I was doing everything right. I could well imagine that this was the cause of my sleep disorders and lack of energy. So, the most important medicine was: 'Don't think too much, Madam!' Don't think so much? Okay, I wanted to try it! Next, I received the prescriptions for my Panchakarma treatments. Panchakarma is an Ayurvedic program which uses various methods in harmony with one another to give the body a full and deep cleansing on both the physical and spiritual levels. The doctor fixed the treatments for the next three days, after which he wanted to see me again. A program was created that included oil massages, herbal baths and wraps, and the intake of herbal juices and pills. I was given a schedule and was told where I could pick up my medication three times a day. There was something like a big letterbox at the entrance of the restaurant where the boxes were labelled with our room numbers. There all the guests met before meals to pick up their pills or tonics or to swallow the not very popular ghee. Ghee is clarified butter, which tastes very strange, but in Ayurveda it plays an important role as a remedy. Luckily, I was spared from it, but my medicine was not a taste of honey either. My most unpopular combination was the one of bitter and salty – horrible. But it was meant to be good for the liver, so down it went! Every few days I saw the doctor again; he assessed my pulse and determined the treatments and medicine for the coming days. In the further course of the treatment, I had a laxative day (which was part of the treatment for everyone) and afterwards I had energising treatments like the stamp massage, where small bags are filled with a warm herbal mixture and used to massage the body. My absolute favourite treatments were the synchronised massages: I was massaged with warm herbal oil by two therapists with perfectly synchronised hand movements. My whole body was treated in this way, with both of the elf-like women working on my body, mirroring each other on each side; then, one moved to work on my head and the other worked on my feet. In order for the medicinal oil to penetrate deep into the skin and connective tissue, their hands stroked, kneaded and tapped for a heavenly whole hour, first in the supine, then in the prone position. I could take this medicine every day! It relaxed my body and brought my mind to rest. After these wonderful oil massages, I felt as if I was made of oil myself, or perhaps like honey – soft, liquid, and completely relaxed. This could not be topped even by the forehead oil treatment, the famous Shirodhara, which is also prescribed to almost every spa guest. If you have ever heard of Ayurveda, then you have most likely heard about this treatment. Women with flowers and oil in their hair decorate the covers of our health magazines again and again. The oil flows in a steady stream from a clay pot to the middle of the forehead, the area corresponding to the third eye. This has an extremely calming effect on the entire nervous system. Some of the other women told me that they lost any sense of time and space during the treatment, which was very liberating and relaxing. There was a lot of talk about it and the expectations of some of them were so high that they could not really relax at all. And then the whole thing was for nothing. I could enjoy it, but I liked the synchronous treatments even more. With all the massages, steam and herbal baths, and sweating in the ayurvedic sauna, the mornings were filled up well; in the afternoon, it was time to relax. This was just as important as the treatments. We went to the sauna – yes, you read that correctly, the tropical climate alone was not enough. In the Svedana, there were two saunas where we were allowed to sweat even more than usual. There, medicinal herbs, which were lying on the floor of the clay igloo, exuded their active ingredients. After the sweating cure I felt like I was made of chewing gum - or ghee: butter-soft. It was really nice - provided you like to sweat. This kind of sauna is by no means available in every Ayurveda hotel, as I learned later. Thus, the sauna became the reason behind the name of the hotel, as the word Svedana means sweating cure.

With yoga in the morning and evening as well as meditations, we additionally purified our body and mind. In doing so, we brought movement to the rusty bodies and calm to the overactive mind. In the afternoon, I had time for swimming in the pool or for walks on the nearby beach. The hotel itself was located at a very special place: there was no beach, but there was a coral reef in front of it. This held back the surf and formed a natural calm pool with sea water. Of course, I found this much nicer than the chlorinated water of the pool. I loved to drift in this warm protected pool and to simply be. When I had more energy again, I made small trips to nearby Galle, where there is an old fort from the time of the Portuguese occupation in the sixteenth century. Or I took the tuktuk to a beach for a walk and visited Buddhist temples. Just riding in the tuktuk was fun – a tuktuk is a vehicle with three wheels and a two-stroke engine, similar to a moped. It gets its name from the noise it makes: tuktuktuktuktuk... With a front seat for the driver and a back seat for three or more Sri Lankans (or two slim Europeans), they are the main means of transport on the island. They are available in different versions all over Asia, and they make the streets look so vibrant, because they come in different colours. Although they all have a canopy made of fabric, they are open at the sides. So, you are immersed in all the smells and noises that the surroundings offer. That includes exhaust fumes and dust, but also the music from the temples, the honking of the buses and the whole cacophony of life in an Asian country. These things are terribly unstable, because they have a high centre of gravity, and easily tip over. Accidents happen all the time. Moreover, their walls are thin like cardboard and offer little resistance when pressed against a tree or a bus. But, in Sri Lanka you should not be afraid, because then you won't ever go out on the road. There would be many ways to die. I never thought about possible dangers, even if I bought something to eat at the roadside – every travel guide advises against it because of the danger of swallowing bacteria. Nothing ever happened to me in this respect on any of my trips to Sri Lanka. I always had confidence in my gut feeling where it was okay - and a strong digestion. At the end of my retreat at the Hotel Svedana, I could not resist, despite good food at the hotel, and went to a restaurant for dinner. I wanted to treat myself to something special, something that every tourist here wants to eat. You might guess what it is. During the remaining days I strictly followed the doctor's orders, as I wanted to get healthy. In the hotel we were spoiled three times a day with delicious and rich buffets. The food was an important part of our treatment, as food is considered to be medicine in Ayurveda. The selection was huge and everything was always very lovingly decorated. Based on the prescription of the doctors, you could choose from many dishes; there were vegetarian curries, but also chicken. And, of course, many exotic fruits like mango, mangosteen, passion fruit, guava, bananas, and even puddings and creams for dessert. Everything your heart could desire - but no seafood! And that's exactly what I treated myself to on my last day. They say that the kind of protein in seafood is hard to digest and also increases the fire in the body. Most of us had only just regulated this fire down, because many of us arrived at the cure stressed and overheated. I wanted to try to keep my elements in balance even after my return, but just one treat couldn't do any harm! So, before my return flight, I let my heart win over my head and enjoyed a large portion of jumbo-prawns with lots of garlic butter and french fries. And, to start the meal off, I allowed myself a gin and tonic, a thing that was also prohibited in the hotel. A divine meal! Everything went down well; my stomach was now healthy and strong and easily coped with this challenge.

In the hotel there were, as I said, lectures in the evenings, so that we also understood what we were experiencing during the program – and also with the lofty goal that we would change a few bad habits at home in order to keep our newly-acquired balance. After all, prevention is better than a cure! The German hostesses translated the melodic Indian English for us, for which many guests were grateful. I enjoyed listening to these lectures. Gradually, I got to know the other guests and after the lectures we sat together with a cup of herbal tea and exchanged our experiences - and sometimes even whole life stories. There were mostly women there; the few men really stood out; I think they were there for the sake of their partners. I can imagine that daily oil massages plus abstinence from alcohol are not the epitome of vacation ideals for most men. With the women, I was amazed at how many repeat visitors there were: some of them seemed to come to the Svedana every year and were totally enthusiastic about it. They told me they felt like a new woman every time they came back. I was curious. All kinds of complaints had brought them here and I was amazed to hear the improvements they had already experienced. High blood pressure had been cured and even insulin-dependent diabetes had improved. I found this very encouraging and was looking forward to telling my patients at home about it.

I really enjoyed the time. Except for small excursions, I had little desire to explore the country. To see Sri Lanka, I knew I could come back again. I concentrated entirely on my recovery. The time flew by, which was certainly helped by the steady flow of the days. I really felt carried through time, not having to organise, plan, or do anything. It was done, I was made well. On the last day, the flower bath, the crowning, no, blooming conclusion of my cure was on the agenda. A bathtub was filled with lukewarm water and then lovingly decorated with flowers. A true work of art awaited me when I entered the room. The whole water surface as well as the edge of the tub were densely decorated with a profusion of different coloured flowers, as only exist in the tropics. I recognised lotuses, water lilies, jasmine, hibiscus and various orchids. The picture was completed with candles, which bathed the room in soft, flickering light. As I stood in front of my flower bath, I was completely overwhelmed by the beauty and love that shone towards me. Tears were running down my cheeks. All this had been made especially for me! It took me a lot of effort to destroy this carpet of flowers, so I climbed very slowly into the water that had cooled down in the meantime. After my chest was covered with flowers again, an employee took some photos of me. What a great end to my retreat! I could hardly believe that time had passed so quickly. And I still remember very well that I fished some lotus flowers out of the bath water at the end and took them back to my room. In the evening I stood by the sea and prayed. I prayed to Buddha to bring me back to this place where I was so happy and felt so blissful. Then I offered him my flowers and threw them into the sea. With this ritual, I expressed a deep heart wish and I am sure it helped to finally make it come true. For I was to return to the land of my dreams, over and over again ... until I no longer needed it.

CHAPTER 7:

New Attempt

Back in Switzerland, I was as good as new: I had lost a little weight, was enthusiastic about Asian cuisine and even bought ghee for cooking because it was so healthy. I also bought cumin, turmeric, curry leaves, mustard seeds and other spices, because I was determined to continue eating healthy food. This good resolution, which probably everyone returning from Ayurveda retreats brings with them, was not really implemented by me for long. But the things I learned then still influence my diet today. What increases the fire in the body? Red wine, beef, seafood, coffee, and sour fruits like pineapple and tomatoes. You should avoid all this during the hot season; however in winter, it is good medicine to get rid of a cold! I have a tendency to be a bit airy-fairy, so I learned what helped me stay grounded: ghee and good oil, both in food and on my body! A few times at home, I actually heated up sesame oil and rubbed it on myself. It was supposed to soak in for twenty minutes, but after ten minutes spent oily and naked in the bathroom, I felt half frozen, so I showered myself off again for a long time with lots of hot water and soap. The climate in Sri Lanka had been much better suited for this sort of treatment. I returned to my husband, my practice, and the daily routine, which - also for a short time - was supplemented by yoga exercises. Discipline is still not my strength!

Walter and I only had a few friends in our hometown and were very much attached to each other. I think we were each other's anchor, which we needed in this strange environment. Neither of us really felt at home there yet. My husband, as the introverted one, was happy about my extroversion, which was, however, paired with an enormous shyness. My two sides. In short, we were often just us two alone; only one very good pair of friends (also German-Swiss) lived nearby. Their daughter was my godchild and we saw each other often. Then there were some acquaintances and Walter's friends in Zurich, whom he visited from time to time. We both earned well, had a nice apartment, a new car and were in our mid/late thirties. The subject of having children of our own kept coming up: my husband didn't want any, and I was torn. In the end, we didn't have any. We went hiking and took bicycle tours, discovered Switzerland and were really happy together. However, there was a problem that increasingly limited these moments of happiness: I simply had no energy. I always wanted to lie down, felt too weak to stand, sometimes even to sit. I had little motivation to do anything. Seeing clients in practice became more and more like torture. I had so many enquiries that I could not possibly accept all of them. So, I brought a friend on board and we worked together in the practice. Luckily, the apartment was big enough and each of us had our own treatment room. We could now represent each other on vacation and on weekends, which gave me more freedom and time to relax. Nevertheless, it was as if my flame of life slowly went out. I no longer had any joy in anything, nor any strength for visitors. Everything was too much for me. So often we had something planned and I had to cancel it, because I simply did not have the strength for it. I was ashamed, I pondered over the reasons, I was desperate. I could not sleep at night, or nap during the day. I felt empty and needy. Yes, needy is the right word. My husband had to take care of me like a sick child. We were no longer man and wife: we were sometimes best friends, sometimes father and daughter. Neither of us was really comfortable. I looked for help, I tried many things. Of course, I had great hope in homeopathy, because I myself worked with it. I had different therapists and many homeopathic remedies, but never felt that any of them really helped. I found a very good kinesiologist who accompanied me for many years and became a good friend. Together, we found themes I worked on, childhood trauma, a lot of sadness. There were food intolerances - I changed my diet. I did not feel better. I went to a dentist; all amalgam fillings were removed, teeth were extracted, I spent a fortune - in Switzerland, no health insurance company pays for this. After kinesiological testing, the dentist gave me minerals, vitamins and all sorts of other things. This also cost money and did not help at all. Walter and I finally did something that many people do in their desperation: in the hope of a new beginning, we decided to move. Maybe the place just wasn't the right one for us. I could not imagine myself as a northern light in the mountains. We drove by car and on our bikes through the surroundings and looked for a nice place. My clear wish was to be by the water. Finally, we found a building site near Lake Sempach, west of Lucerne. The architect was still looking for buyers and had just started building a six-family complex. We decided to buy an apartment there. We could still move walls, design the bathroom, choose tiles, the flooring, the kitchen. There was a lot to decide, it was fun - but it was also a colossal burden for me. I simply had too little energy to be really happy. We moved into our dream apartment in 2002, four years after I had experienced my treatment in Sri Lanka, five years after I started my practice. I would have to commute to work, but by train it was only about forty-five minutes. So, with a lot of hope we moved to Sempach. Again, a new beginning!

CHAPTER 8:

It Can't Go On Like This

Unfortunately, the move to Lake Sempach did not improve my energy level in any way. The solution was not that simple. I soon didn't sleep at all, not for a single minute. I wandered through the days like a zombie, constantly waiting for the moment when I could finally go to bed. I had a glass of wine in the evening, and my heart was pounding all night long. Little by little I also tried all the natural remedies, from valerian pills to lavender balm, orange blossom tea, Bach flowers, Schüssler salts and so on. Finally, I took a sleeping pill, and today I thank heaven that this did not help either. With it, I was able to sleep a single night passably, but the following night was a torture as before, despite the pill. I threw the sleeping pills away. There came a moment when I had to admit to myself that I could not take this anymore. I think we had only been in our dream apartment for six months. How could I help people in this condition? I took a sick leave and was diagnosed with exhaustion depression. I found a fill-in for the practice and could now be at home and take care of myself:

go for a walk when I found the strength to do so, swim in the lake, give space to my own therapies. It was liberating. Thanks to a daily allowance insurance, I even received money for my loss of earnings until I was summoned by a medical examiner after three months. The psychiatrist talked to me for an hour and assessed me as fit for work. I should go back to work and earn my own money again. This was a shock, because even after three months of rest I was not able to do so. One morning I got up with the clear realisation: I must give up my practice! Walter and I were desperate. After all, we had just taken out a loan to finance our apartment and had expected regular income. But it was now really clear: this was not the way to go on. With a heavy heart I informed my patients and invited them to my practice for a farewell party. Many came, all of them were sad and brought me recovery wishes and loving cards. And I was sad at first, it was horrible! I loved my practice, and I had also built a heart-to-heart relationship with my clients, and I left there reluctantly. It was also the final farewell to the place where I had lived for seven years. It was raining, it was a grey day and I was completely depressed. From that day on I had no daily structure at all, no goal, no hope. I hung out alone in our beautiful new apartment and waited for my husband to come home from work. Unforgotten is an evening when I had struggled to cook dinner and my husband wanted some grated cheese. I put a bag of cheese on the table, he sprinkled it over his food, and the cheese was mouldy. His meal was ruined. That sounds like a small thing, but I remember the normally quiet man ran out of patience and he said something like, 'Can't you get anything done?' We were both at the end of our rope. I did what I could, but I didn't feel any better. I'm still grateful to Walter for not letting me down during that time. And

I have to say that if I look back today, I would prescribe myself an antidepressant for a while. But at the time, that wasn't an option for me.

So, Walter and I lived side by side, unhappy, hopeless and helpless. We honestly could think of nothing more that would help me. We needed a miracle. It was clear that we had to separate, because it was very exhausting to live together like this. But neither of us moved. There was not enough money for a second apartment, and I felt too weak to do anything. Then one day a higher power intervened again; I can't call it anything else. I was led, and it was Sri Lanka again that called me. And this is how it happened: I was on a bus trip to Sursee, to go for a little stroll. On the way back, we stopped at a traffic light and I looked out: a man crossed the road in front of us. He had brown skin and dark hair. For me, it was immediately clear that he had to come from Sri Lanka. And then suddenly there was a cascade of thoughts. As if they were dominos, one word led to another: Sri Lanka, Ayurveda hotel, German tour, guest relations. And suddenly I knew, crystal clear, what my next step would be: I wanted to travel to Sri Lanka and work at the Hotel Svedana as a guest guide! Today I still feel the shiver of goose bumps that overflowed me. It felt so right, so fitting, so saving. Strangely enough, I never doubted for a moment that I would have enough energy to survive the long journey and do this job. I hurried home and looked on the internet for the information I was looking for: the hotel was owned by a Sri Lankan but was exclusively marketed by a German company. This company also hired the German hostesses. Their job was to translate during the doctor's consultations and lectures and to be there for the guests. They had the lofty title GRO, Guest Relations Officer. During my stay at Svedana, I met two of them and had a picture of what I would have to do. I applied to the German company, which was based near Munich. There I was allowed to introduce myself the following week and was asked whether I could imagine teaching yoga. Although I had no training in this direction, I felt fit for it, as I had been practicing it myself for years. A trained local yoga teacher would demonstrate the exercises and I would explain and accompany the guests. I thought I could do that. Two weeks later I received the promise and my prayer was fulfilled: I was allowed to return to Sri Lanka. Even to the same place where I had held my ceremony. It was indeed a miracle! I was inspired by hope and joy and my energy increased a little bit. My contract came by mail soon after. It ran for six months and it was planned that after this time my husband would come to Sri Lanka and we would spend a holiday together. These prospects filled me with great joy and new energy. Life had taken on new colours again and I could already smell the scent of curry and the air of the tropics. I was of some use after all!

CHAPTER 9:

Where is Your Husband?

The following half year brought many new experiences for me. It was something completely different, working in a hotel as opposed to spending holidays there. There was a lot to discover behind the scenes and not everything was easy. I took great pleasure in accompanying people through the treatments and advising them when they wanted to make excursions. The Ayurveda treatments at the Hotel Svedana were Panchakarma treatments that purify the body, but also the psyche would become clearer and lighter. Often, the removal of physical waste products is accompanied by detoxification on the emotional level. Old injuries, anger, grief, loneliness and other spirits show their heads and there are real blue days when tears are shed in abundance. I had experienced it myself. During those times, you're happy if you have someone to listen to you; I knew this from my own experience too. I also liked this part of my work, because I had experience in it from my own practice: I offered our guests my ear and my shoulder and surprisingly, I had the necessary energy for it again.

I myself also lived in the hotel building; on the top floor there were a few rooms for employees who had to stay there overnight. For our guests, there should always be someone available who spoke German. I worked six days a week, with only one day off. Strictly forbidden to have private contact with the local staff of the hotel, I was allowed to spend my free time only with the other German hostess – not with the Sri Lankan staff. If we were only seen in the same bus, there was talk, and quickly, a warning. I experienced this once, when I was on the road on my day off. I was glad to see one of the waiters from the restaurant on the way to Galle, whom I saw every day at work, and I approached him full of joy. He behaved strangely dismissive and at first, I did not know why. But the very next day, the whole hotel was gossiping about us having 'something' together. Which was not true! A warning from the management was missing this time – we were lucky. Of course, this was also a sensitive issue for the mostly female spa guests: they could not be forbidden to have contact with the staff, but it was clearly communicated that it was undesirable. And the employees were indeed threatened with immediate dismissal if such a case became known. Another guest attendant was thrown out years later because of her relationship with a porter. She has been married for years now to her Sri Lankan boyfriend from that time, and both of them fortunately found new jobs. But this does not always turn out so happily for the local staff and large families who depend on their income. The guests (and we) were also warned about the so-called beach boys. This group of Sri Lankans stays near tourist spots and tries to do business: excursions for sale, shells, traditional wooden masks, Ayurvedic oils, all very cheap, Madam! Often a friendly relationship develops, addresses are exchanged, and the Sri Lankans very much hope that one stays in contact. And maybe even send a few Euros. Some boys could be quite pushy and persuasive and this became very exhausting and stressful for the guest. Therefore, we were all advised against close contact, which was not difficult for me. Some women, on the other hand, were of course looking for just that: close contact, but in a physical sense. I had not known until then that there is a lively sex tourism in Sri Lanka, where middle-aged women, often divorced and hungry for love and connection, come to find local men to satisfy those needs, even just for a few nights. The hotel management was of course aware of this, and to protect the visitors who were there for Ayurvedic healing and not looking for such a relationship, clear boundaries were drawn. These were understandable rules in this respect, but they made it very difficult for me to find someone with whom I could spend my free time - even without sexual ulterior motives. I lived in Sri Lanka, worked six days a week, lived in a hotel and was not allowed to have contact with the people there. Somehow, I had a picture in my mind of a Gallic village surrounded by Romans, like in the Asterix and Obelix comics. My hotel was the Gallic village, an island surrounded by enemies. Were the locals really that bad? There was another German who worked with me, but of course we both never had our day off at the same time. In the evenings, either she had to translate or I did, and our days off were staggered too. So, I was once again alone. My small salary was good enough to live on; food and accommodation were paid by the hotel. But soon I started to spend my days off in a hotel in Unawatuna, a popuar destination on the coast near Galle, where I was incognito and where I could be a tourist. I also wanted to walk around lightly dressed and be undisturbed. So, most of my money was spent on that and on the visits to restaurants outside the hotel. But it was no problem, I was fine. My energy increased constantly, and I could sleep better, felt healthier and stronger. My decision to come to Sri Lanka had been right.

Over time, despite the isolation, I learned many interesting things about the country I now lived in. Life in Sri Lanka is characterised by a network of relationships. Many Sri Lankans are poor, many have no regular income. So, money to buy something is not always in the house. On the other hand, there are many obligations that a family has to meet: if you go to a wedding, you bring money. For the New Year, you buy new clothes for yourself and for others: a new sarong, a new dress or shorts. The families are very large, and everyone has to be taken into account. If a child is born in the family or neighbourhood, it costs money; funerals cost even more. Ceremonies have to be held, monks invited, guests need food and drink. When a girl has her first menstrual period, a rite of passage known as a big girl party occurs, which is often attended by at least a hundred people. And then, of course, there is the wedding, the highlight of every woman's life (I find it hard to estimate what the male equivalent would be). A wedding celebration in Sri Lanka takes several days, requires two different locations and many festive dresses and means catering for hundreds of guests. It is a mystery to me how even people with an income can pay for this, but if you don't have a paid job, it seems almost impossible. At full moon, offerings are made in the temple to Lord Buddha, who is satisfied with lotus flowers or jasmine blossoms, an oil lamp and incense sticks. Since a Hindu deity is often also worshipped on the same temple grounds, bowls with fruits and flower garlands are also bought in addition to the temple offerings in order to make them gracious as well. The people in Sri Lanka are believers, but also superstitious. They fear the wrath of the gods and also their unfavourable neighbours, who could charge them with black magic. To protect themselves from this, they call upon all available protective deities, whether they are Buddhist or Christian. Double is better. All this costs money. It is true that many things they need to survive grow on trees, but there is no money tree in Sri Lanka. Most of the people are in debt and it takes a wide network of friends and family to lend each other money. Young women and men live with their parents until a spouse is found and they marry. In the rural area in the southwest, which I eventually got to know better, most marriages were arranged by parents and marriage brokers. It was important that the horoscopes of those who wanted to get married matched. Sex before marriage was taboo; a woman had to enter marriage as a virgin. For a long time, there were no divorces at all; now, they are possible, but they can take forever and cost a lot of money. A woman did not live alone – that was completely unthinkable. With the marriage, she moved into the house of the man and his family. When her husband died, she stayed with the husband's parents or moved back to her parents. It was and is completely natural in this culture for children to care for their elderly parents. There is hardly any room for personal needs and self-realisation, which play such a big role in our culture. Privacy is unknown. Sri Lankans are never alone and feel most comfortable in groups; they aren't used to solitude and don't generally long to be on their own sometimes. All the more strange to them must seem women from the West travelling alone. And so, the most frequently asked question of me was, 'Where is your husband?', followed by, 'How many children do you have?'

I rescued myself during this time with the answer, 'Husband working, coming later.' In the beginning I kept to the truth about the number of children, but after seeing the deep pity in the eyes of the questioner when I said 'No children', I switched to white lies. Depending on the day, my number of children fluctuated between one and three. They were looked after at home by their grandmother during my absence. Because there are women in Sri Lanka who work far away from their home, children left with grandmothers was a situation they were familiar with. Some even commit themselves to work as housemaids in Arab countries for more than two years and leave their children with the family. Work is hard to find on the island, especially for women. There are some textile factories in the south, there are hotels where they can clean. But they do not earn much money there. Everyone was happy with my answer, I fit in with the familiar patterns. And that was mostly what we talked about, because not all Sri Lankans speak English. The women very seldom did. I phoned once a week with my husband in Switzerland. We didn't have Skype yet, so for six months I could only hear him, not see him. In the beginning I was homesick, of course, and the time seemed to last forever. But when I was halfway through, the clock ran much faster and I could honestly say, 'Husband coming soon.' Walter and I had planned to make a two-week road trip and I greatly enjoyed planning it. Until it was finally time: my husband came to Sri Lanka!

CHAPTER 10:

Surprise

In the weeks before Walter's arrival I had a strange feeling, despite all the joy: somehow, there was a distance in our phone calls. He seemed reserved. Was it just the way he acted? Was he excited and unable to show his joy? It was just a faint hunch, but I was happy to ignore it. I can no longer remember if I ever asked him what was going on. He flew to Sri Lanka and I went with the driver to Colombo to pick him up. For the first few nights, I had rented a hotel bungalow close to the Svedana. Walter should first have time to get used to the tropical climate before we went on the road trip. Of course, I also wanted to show him the hotel where I had spent the last six months and the beautiful surroundings. I had found a really romantic place that would have pleased any honeymoon couple. There was an oval pool from which one could see the sea. An ideal place to catch up on the closeness we hadn't experienced for so long. Or so I thought. But then everything turned out completely different. There was something going on and Walter dropped the bomb on the very first day. He gathered all his courage and confessed to me that he had fallen in love! He had met the woman during a yoga week in Greece. Two months ago. My subconscious had a hunch, but my consciousness was completely exhausted. He felt miserable about the situation; of course, he had thought about whether he should come at all. But to end a marriage on the phone was not his style. I broke down completely, cried and cried and cried. In between, we talked. It hurt incredibly and I wanted to understand why he preferred her to me. But what was there to understand? Our relationship had been difficult for a long time, for years. Whether my illness was the cause or the result, who knows? I cried my eyes out, was violently ill, the world collapsed for me. And we were sitting in Sri Lanka and had a road trip to go on. What now? I was in a miserable state, both emotionally and physically, and could hardly eat. My belly was still restless even after the three days in our honeymoon nest. Nevertheless, we decided to take the road trip anyway. Somehow, I had the hope that I could still change his mind. It was unspeakably exhausting. Since I knew the country and the people better than Walter, it was up to me to organise everything. We saw the well-known highlights at temples and cultural sites like the Temple of the Tooth, in Kandy, a Buddhist temple which houses a precious relic: a tooth of the Buddha. We visited the rock temple in Dambulla, the elephant orphanage in Pinnawala and much more. We stayed in the reserved luxury hotels and went on elephant safari in a jeep. Under different circumstances, it would have been so beautiful! On the way from the national park to our car, we rode in a small boat towards the sunset and again I could not stop crying. The view was so unbelievably beautiful and romantic, but it did not fit our situation at all. At the end of our trip, we landed in

Negombo, north of Colombo, in a beach hotel. Driver and guide were released, and we were alone again. I had already booked my return flight seven months ago, Walter booked his at short notice, and unfortunately, we could not travel back in the same plane. His flight was in two days, I had to spend another five days alone in paradise. I called the airline; a rebooking was not possible. It was high season in Sri Lanka and all flights were fully booked. I was weak and my stomach still could hardly stand more than rice and cooked vegetables, and so I comforted myself with the fact that I needed the days to make myself fit to fly. Those days were hell! I was lonely, emotionally hurt, physically weak. Even today tears come to my eyes when I think about it. After Walter's departure, I pulled myself together as best I could and finally followed him: to our condo, into an uncertain future, without a job, with the decision to separate from my husband. To say it was not nice is a massive understatement, but I lack the words for the misery I felt at that time. I called my family in Hamburg and said that Walter and I were going to separate. From their side, I experienced sympathy - Walter had finally left me. I also felt a certain relief, because they had never been happy with our relationship. They had always felt that we did not fit together, that we were too different. Maybe they were right. And my mother made the suggestion, 'Why don't you come back home?'

Sri Lanka Calling

CHAPTER 11:

Home - Where is That?

But that was exactly my problem: where was my home? My parents had, as already mentioned, moved us around very often. The longest time we had lived anywhere was in a small town near Hamburg, but I had never felt comfortable in the confinement of that small town. And anyway, nobody in my family lived there anymore. My parents had gotten divorced, and they now lived in rented apartments in different cities; my sisters were in Hamburg itself. There was no parental home to which I could have returned. Besides, I had been living in Switzerland for sixteen years and had a few friends there. More than in Germany, anyway. I had withdrawn from everyone during my long illness. Having slept well in Sri Lanka before Walter's arrival, I now fell back into old patterns and dragged myself through the days. I could not imagine moving to Germany in this condition. So, I looked for an apartment in Lucerne, which is only about twenty kilometres away from Sempach. I thought it would be easy to settle in there and also to open a new practice. We divided up our household

(I'll take the table, you can have the sofa) and I packed my things. Walter stayed in Sempach for a few more months until we could sell our apartment. We kept in touch; he was worried about me as always and also felt guilty for the separation. I needed a few more months to come to terms with the situation. From today's point of view, I am infinitely grateful that this woman came between us. Without her, we would probably never have managed the long overdue step of separation. It was the best thing for both of us. By the way, the relationship between Walter and his first girlfriend didn't last long, he is now married to another woman. We have a relaxed, friendly relationship and we see each other occasionally for dinner.

I quickly felt at home in Lucerne. We had visited there often over the years, and many things were familiar to me. Now I lived there in my own three-room apartment. I wanted to have it nice and had bought some new furniture and also a small car, a Mazda. It was metallic green, had a sunroof, and I loved driving it through the beautiful landscape of the Lucerne hinterland. I felt free and everything seemed to be possible again. I also loved to travel on Lake Lucerne. There is a fleet of antique paddle steamers there and, from Lucerne, I took wonderful trips, which always did me a lot of good. There were many places where I could change from a ship to a mountain railway and then I was up in the air in no time without any effort. Mount Rigi alone offers so many possibilities for hiking, walking, or just sitting and enjoying the view. I love Lake Lucerne: the water is crystal clear yet has a beautiful green glow, and the panorama with the surrounding mountains is like a dream. It was nice to be swayed by the rhythm of the ships' engines, and again it was the feeling of travelling that brought me joy. Everything would be good – new and good!

Our divorce had been filed and Walter generously offered to support me financially for a year until I could sort myself out and earn money again. I found a part-time job at a school where doctor-secretaries were trained, and so I had to work at least two evenings a week and earned my own money. After a few months I had the necessary energy and confidence in myself again and started with homeopathic treatments in Lucerne. I rented a room in a community practice and felt very comfortable in the team of therapists. A few former patients found their way to me, but it was a real new beginning, with advertisements and a lot of waiting and hoping - unlike when I opened my first practice, it started very slowly.

At the same time, I was looking for connections to like-minded people, as I had no friends in Lucerne yet. Once again, a great coincidence came to my aid: before my departure from Sri Lanka, I had talked about Buddhism with a guest at the Hotel Svedana; it was a topic which greatly interested both of us. He was in Sri Lanka in search of special temples and the palm leaf library that was frequently talked about. Information about past lives is kept in this library and waits for whoever asks for it. Wise men are said to have seen this information (with their third eye) and recorded it on palm leaves. And in this way, the visitor would receive important information that could help him in his present life. It was hard to imagine, but apparently a reality. I had heard about similar libraries in India but had never met anyone who had found them. This man was eager to learn more about his life's path, his previous lives, and his soul's purpose. I don't know if he found it, because I only saw him that one time. However, in farewell, he gave me the address of a Buddhist centre in Switzerland, saying I should definitely visit it when I was back home. It was in Lucerne, of all places! As I was living there now, I looked for it. And wonder of wonders: it was only a ten-minute walk from my apartment! The Nalanda Centre offered lessons according to the teachings of the Tibetan monk Geshe Kelsang Gyatso. This elderly master has established a worldwide network of New Kadampa Tradition Centres and has written many books on Buddha's teachings. Now living in England after his escape from Tibet, he has adapted the originally secret and difficult texts and practices to our Western lifestyle. His vision is to make this teaching accessible to all people, whether ordained or not, and in this way help them to train their minds. Of course, I had to see this Nalanda, because I trusted that I had not received this advice by chance. After attending a first lecture, I was totally enthusiastic. I have always loved to deal with questions of life and there were plenty of people here who were interested. The other members were friendly and welcomed me, and soon I had a new circle of friends. I was interested in many topics of spiritual training. Among other things, I wanted to understand the influence of past lives on what I experience today. I knew intuitively that this was not my first time on Earth, although I could not remember any previous incarnations. But had I perhaps once lived in Sri Lanka? Is that why the country attracted me so much? I did not receive any answers to these questions during my time in Lucerne. They came to me later in unexpected ways. And I was right! Of course, there were causes in the past that guided my life. That is the law of karma. Here in Lucerne I had only a logical understanding of this cosmic law. Years later, it became very tangible and helped me greatly to accept what I was experiencing. But I'll come to that later. For now, my life in Switzerland continued and Sri Lanka retreated into the background for a while.

What I liked very much, besides studying the books, were our meditations and singing the mantras. This was balm for my soul! So, I joined the program to intensively study the Buddhist teachings and spent at least two evenings a week in the centre. I must have often lived in Buddhist monasteries in previous lives, because it all felt very familiar. Here I had a feeling of home. I spent a total of five years with the dear friends I found at Nalanda, and I still have contact with some of them today. We are connected by many beautiful and intense experiences, both on a spiritual and a friendly level. Together we visited international festivals in Berlin, England, France, and even in Singapore. We did silence retreats in the Swiss mountains and followed the Buddhist calendar with pujas (offerings) and other ceremonies. There was always a lot to organise and one of my favourite tasks was preparing and decorating the altar. The altar was colour coordinated with the Buddha of the day. Blue for the medicine Buddha, green for the green Tara and so on. I have always loved colours and creativity runs through my veins. Back then, I created some real works of art and I always like to look at old photos of my creations.

Another hobby of mine was cooking. Not only for myself alone, but for a group. At the festivals or retreats in Switzerland, we had to cater for ourselves and I liked to volunteer for shopping and cooking. Together with a friend, I then went shopping for tons of food (once, we filled three big shopping carts) and prepared food for twenty to thirty hungry meditators. We ate vegetarian food and I liked to cook according to recipes of the Asian cuisine with tofu and curry, which always went down well. I was actually quite happy. Although I didn't have a partner, wasn't sleeping well, and my practice was going badly, I was very content. It was a rich time and I like to think back on it. My wealth at that time really consisted of the feeling of community; I felt understood and accepted in this group of like-minded people. This kind of connection is priceless! In the hope of becoming even happier and healthier, I continued to see therapists and search for shadows within me. There was a deep darkness and sadness and I wanted to lighten it up. I went to courses with an Irish medium and experienced weekends with shamans and power animals. Still, a mood of heaviness remained, and I never seemed to find the deep reason. In 2005, our divorce was finalised. Between 2004 and 2009, I was in Sri Lanka two more times and was pampered with Ayurveda. Each time, it did me a world of good and I was happy. Each time, I said: 'I feel at home here, I want to live here!' The desire was still very strong. In 2009, I stayed in a small hotel near Galle, a town on the south coast of the island. The hotel belonged to a German couple and offered Ayurveda treatments and eight luxury rooms directly on the beach. I will call it Palm Villa here. Also, there were German guest attendants who took care of the guests' wellbeing. It was a very familiar small group that came together there and I felt completely comfortable. I also had some personal conversations with Margrit, who owned this little paradise and who occasionally accompanied me during my walks on the beach. She was an open ear and shoulder to me, and I felt that I had found in her a friend who understood and appreciated me. After I had finished my usual ritual with the lotus flowers and prayer, Please, Buddha, bring me back to Sri Lanka, I travelled back to Switzerland. This was in October 2009.

CHAPTER 12:

New Year Greetings and an Invitation

The year 2010 dawned. As usual, I had slept through New Year's Eve. I am not a night owl and I like to spend the transition of the year contemplatively, saying goodbye to the old year and formulating wishes and plans for the new one. How could I have guessed that this year would change my life fundamentally! If I'd had any inkling of what was to come, I would probably not have been able to sleep at all that night. It was the third of January when I received a special call. Area code 0094 ... Who is calling me from Sri Lanka? My heart began racing. It was Margrit, the owner of the Palm Villa. She asked if I had received the email she had sent me. I was flabbergasted – New Year's greetings? No, I hadn't seen anything. She promised to resend the email right away. I waited anxiously for the ping of the mailbox and devoured her words:

Dear Kerstin, Wolfgang and I would be delighted if you would come to the Palm Villa and work with us. During your last visit we took you to our hearts and we offer you the vacant job of guest caretaker.

I couldn't believe it. Really?! Was this a joke? I was so excited! The email went on: my job would involve doing what I had done years before at the Hotel Svedana, namely, looking after the well-being of the guests. I would welcome them when they arrived from the airport exhausted, accompany them to the doctor's consultations, organise excursions, guide meditations and much more. In addition, I would organise the bookings, communicate with the guests, and supervise the local staff in the housekeeping and restaurant. A diversified task, which I would carry out together with a German colleague. I could start in May; they would get me a visa with which I could stay in Sri Lanka for a year. And, once again, they expressed how overjoyed they would be for me to join them! I was speechless, breathless, overwhelmed, my heart almost jumped out of my chest! My wish of many years seemed to be coming true: I had a chance to live in the country of my heart and work directly on the beach of the Indian Ocean. It was immediately clear to me that I would take this chance and leave. Give up my practice, which was not going well anyway. Leave my apartment, emigrate. This would be my second emigration, after I had already come from Germany to Switzerland. I took a few more days to think about it and kept checking in with myself, but the good feeling, that great unbridled joy, did not get weaker. Yes, I wanted to travel! I wanted to start a new life in the tropics, surrounded by loving people, to finally be happy and at home. I was often asked then and again later whether I was not afraid. To be honest: I was never afraid. It just felt right.

A few days later, I received a second call, this time from Zurich. I was at home in my apartment when the phone rang.

Dr Kerstin Joost

It was the supervisor in charge of the department of the health insurance company I had been working at for three years. I did this work in addition to my practical work. This meant that I travelled to Zurich three days a week to advise insured persons on medical questions over the phone. Night and weekend services were also part of this, but I was able to do these from home. It was a job that I enjoyed, also because I was free in the content of my consultations: I was allowed to give recommendations that I could stand behind and was not restricted to orthodox medicine. It was also great to work here in a team, because in my practice I was often alone. My boss was now on the phone and wanted to discuss something with me. He knew me very well, because I had been one of the first doctors to work on this new project, and we had set the ball rolling together. He had a great suggestion for me: 'Kerstin, we have to make a change and need a new head for the department. We thought of you. Would you do it?' I was totally surprised – I had actually gotten a second job offer within a week! And they could not have been more different from one another. If I were to go the way of the health insurance company, I could have a career, gain a lot of new experience in a leading position and also earn good money. Especially compared to the salary I would get in Sri Lanka. In Sri Lanka, an adventure was waiting for me, an opportunity that sounded like the fulfilment of my long-time dreams. Now I had to decide what I wanted to follow: my head or my heart, reason or feeling? I asked him for two days to think it over, although I had actually already made up my mind long ago: heart over head! To confirm this, I quickly met up with a woman whom I had already asked for advice several times previously: she worked with tarot cards. I asked her what she would advise me to do, and her answer was clear: 'Sri Lanka is calling for you, go there! Follow your heart. There you will also find your soul mate. He is waiting under a palm tree!' That was exactly what I wanted to hear, and my decision was final: I would go to Sri Lanka and work in the Ayurveda hotel. And so, I told my boss: 'Sorry, I'm not taking the promotion. And,' clearing my throat, 'uh, I quit!' It was weird. He regretted my decision very much and described the dilemma he was dealing with: my direct superior had some health issues, and it was decided that she would need to be released from work. Therefore, they needed a successor immediately. Would I take over the job ad interim while I was still in Switzerland? I had to give a period of notice anyway and would still be there for a while. I was flattered and didn't want to let him down, so I agreed to do the three months. Oh, my God! When I think about the time today, I can't imagine for the life of me how I did it all. There was a lot to do at the company. I was allowed to process things that had been left under the management of my unwell predecessor. All of a sudden, I was chairing meetings and making decisions – as always – with full commitment and at a fast German pace. Fortunately, I only worked part-time, so there was still time for my private affairs, i.e. the selling of my belongings. I decided to keep as little as possible and let go of almost everything. I saw no possibility to store my things, because in Switzerland even the rent for a cellar room costs a fortune and I would earn little in Sri Lanka. I could put some boxes in the cellar at a friend's place, for free, but that was it. I sold all the furniture from both my apartment and practice online or gave it away to the Buddhist centre, who were very happy with it. I even held a small flea market in the office, bringing many things like clothes, books, knickknacks, lamps, and so on to new owners. That was fun! A colleague from

Lucerne helped me to transport my things and I was allowed to use a vacant office in our department where I spread everything out. During the lunch break and after work, colleagues came by and took whatever they could use. I received two francs here, five there, and I got rid of a lot. It may sound careless, but I can let go of material things easily. I then look forward to the new things that I will certainly have soon. (I have more trouble letting go of people.) I made good progress. My homeopathic medicines, all in the form of sugar globules in small glass bottles, were given to a homeopath from Lucerne, and united our heartfelt relationship with Sri Lanka: after the 2004 tsunami, she had set up an aid project to send homeopathic medicines to support those who were affected. The traumatised people needed help and there were many physical wounds to heal and infections to cure. She had found local therapists and built a small centre in the northeast of the island. Over the following year, my medicines went there in portions of two kilos in the luggage of some of her friends. Hopefully they helped many people. I gave them away; in Switzerland, there would have been nothing more to do with opened medicine bottles anyway. In Sri Lanka, however, they were worth their weight in gold. That went on my positive karma account!

And so the months flew by. There was a lot to organise, such as terminating health insurance, electricity and telephone, deregistration at the residents' registration office, and a thousand other things. For the deregistration, I had to pay my taxes first, which meant that I had to do my tax return before that. A complicated task! I was glad when I had finally done everything. To clean my apartment, I afforded myself the luxury of a good fairy, namely, a cleaner. In Switzerland, handing over an apartment is a very tricky business. Every corner is checked for immaculate cleanliness and it may be that on the day of the move you have to clean a blind because it is not clean enough for the caretaker. I was very happy that I didn't have to take care of it and was happy to pay for it. A neighbour was glad to do this and earn the money. Then I urgently needed a new tenant; I could only terminate my tenancy agreement in six months. So, I stuck a note on the front door and looked for interested parties. If I could suggest even one suitable candidate, I got out of the contract by the end of the day. And again, something very special happened: the very same evening the phone rang, and a family wanted to come round. They lived nearby and were glad that they were allowed to come to my house to have a first look. When I opened the door, words failed me: the brown skin, the slim figure ... they clearly came from India ... or ... Sri Lanka? Right! They were Tamils from Colombo! We laughed out loud when I said I was going to emigrate to the country they came from. They hadn't been there for a few years though, and the children hardly knew the country. It was too funny! They asked me to put in a good word for them with the administration, which I of course gladly did. And indeed, they got the lease and became my next tenants. It was a joy on both sides! They invited me to their house for dinner and prepared me for my new home with rice and curry. Of course, I was picked up by car and brought back home, full service all around. I saw it as another good omen, Sri Lanka was calling me! At some point, the last working day was over and we had a drink at the company to say goodbye. Everyone was sad but envied me for my freedom and courage. However, most of them would have declined such an offer and felt comfortable where they were. I spent the last days before my flight in a small guest house on Lake Lucerne. I had a room with a view over the lake and mountains and was in need of some rest, because I was completely exhausted and had massive sleep problems again. Once again, I had done too much. It was an intense time and, although I was sure in my decision, I was still nervous. This time it wasn't just for six months, this time it was ... forever?! I said goodbye to Switzerland and travelled to Sri Lanka, the country like no other, on the 30th of April 2010. A new chapter of my life began. A dream came true.

Sri Lanka Calling

CHAPTER 13:

Welcome to Sri Lanka

Something I will always remember when I think of Sri Lanka is the moment when the glass door at the airport opened and I stepped out of the air conditioning into the tropical heat. That moment was divine; I can't explain it any other way: I crashed into a wall of warm and humid air saturated with exotic smells. There were flowers, dust, earth, burnt garbage, exhaust fumes, overripe fruits and much more. Add to this the typical sounds of the native birds and I feel a deep nostalgia and longing at the thought of this combination. It felt like coming home this time too and I was completely happy, no matter how tired I was. The driver of the Palm Villa picked me up and we arrived safely at our destination after the usual crawl. My employers themselves lived on the premises of the hotel, but for their German employees they rented a house which was very close by. It was newly renovated and Margrit had furnished it with much love. Besides me, another woman was living there at that time and she showed me my room, which was almost completely filled with the typical dark brown four-poster bed with mosquito netting. There was also a large common living room full of designer furniture, and a shower room. The kitchen was huge, but empty. We could eat in the hotel as part of our room and board. I hardly had time to look at all of it, as I was picked up for dinner. Directly on the beach, a table was set and for my welcome party we sat barefoot with four of us under the starry sky and raised our wine glasses to a nice time and good cooperation. I had arrived. 'Sawdiya puramu - Cheers!'

I think I only had one day to acclimatise and adjust to the local time, and then my work started. Sri Lanka is three and a half hours ahead of Switzerland in summer and four and a half in winter. The physical adjustment took me about a week each time, but I felt quite fit. I already knew the hotel, but from the perspective of a guest. Now, I was allowed to look behind the scenes and was introduced to the work on the computer, where I answered emails in the cool breeze of the air conditioner. I loved to welcome the mostly female guests and to give them as much attention as I had always gotten myself. Everyone arrived pale and exhausted and blossomed visibly under the great pampering program. Heartwarming to see and fantastic to experience for yourself! When I started to work at the Palm Villa, there was a problem with the Ayurveda doctor on whom the whole process of the hotel depended. He showed a clear disinterest in his work, came in later and later and left earlier and earlier. It was probably not his dream job to treat exhausted Europeans. Margrit and Wolfgang wanted him to leave the hotel as soon as possible, as his bad mood and work morale was spreading to the rest of the team of therapists and employees. The only problem was: no doctor, no treatments! A doctor has to do the initial and final examinations and prescribe the treatments to be used during the program. They are more or less always the same treatments, but the medicines and oils vary according to the type of constitution and the illness. So, we urgently needed a new doctor. I still have to laugh today when I think that I played a key role in that moment - and dug my own grave at the same time. It started like this: through my repeated visits to Sri Lanka, I knew a few people who worked in Ayurveda hotels. I visited with them and felt wonderfully integrated into the local network; then, suddenly, a doctor contacted me: she had heard on the grapevine that I had a job to offer. She was very keen to know if I would be interested in her working for us. I was already practically a local, I already had the right connections! She introduced herself to us and actually got the job. We all immediately found her very nice and committed, the exact opposite of the grumpiness we had to deal with up to now. The treatments could continue and we could make our guests happy, the way it should be! I felt like a valuable member of the Palm Villa team.

And I felt comfortable in that little hotel. The work was familiar to me, I knew most of the employees and the mentality as well. The first few weeks it was murderously hot. In May, the monsoon season usually starts, and until then, the thermometer rises almost daily. Even though it is always at least 30 degrees, a few degrees more and a higher humidity make a big difference. We could hardly move and avoided the direct sun like the plague. The hotel had a pool that was of course reserved for the guests. But when everybody was busy with their treatments, we guest attendants and the bosses also jumped in for a short time. I love pools, I would say I am a real pool-addict: the colour of the water makes my soul cheer and I can bask in it for hours. The sea, on the other hand, looks inviting, but is treacherous in Sri Lanka: especially on the south-west coast, there are many undercurrents, and sea-bathing is often dangerous. Again and again, foreign guests drown, and Sri Lankans can only be seen in the water where it is really calm and protected, like in a lagoon or behind a reef. Most locals never learn to swim, because they have no access to swimming pools! White people only. So, I felt really privileged to be allowed to use our pool and did so as often as I could. I was very much appreciated by Margrit and Wolfgang; they were visibly happy that I was there. And I think they also had the idea that the presence of a German doctor would have a positive effect on the turnover of their hotel. Since our Ayureda doctor had never treated foreign guests before, she needed some training. I was very happy to do this. Dealing with sick people is different in Sri Lanka than in Europe: there is a rough tone and also the treatments are less gentle. We are not used to this and need the velvet glove version. So, I showed Dr. Ruvini how our German guests wanted to be welcomed and how she could question them. I taught her English and German vocabulary like, 'Lie on your stomach!' or, 'You can get dressed.' We worked out a questionnaire which we filled out together with the guest during the admission interview: which previous illnesses existed, which medications were taken, and so on. At first it went really well, and it felt like we were a strong team. Dr. Ruvini was infinitely grateful that I got her the job, because she needed money to send her daughter to an international school. This dream had now come true and she was shining like the sun.

At least for a couple of weeks, everything was fine. But somehow and sometime a shadow crept into this apparent paradise. I can't say how it started, maybe there was no single event that made the difference. Maybe Dr. Ruvini was well enough trained by now and was firmly enough in the saddle. My feeling was that the Ayurvedic doctor saw me as a competitor. After all, as a doctor I was a respected person, just like her. Ayurveda doctors often come from a family of doctors who pass on their knowledge and skills to the following generations, the knowledge of life, as Ayurveda is translated. They are traditional and very proud, everyone in Sri Lanka treats them with great respect. Of course, I also respected them, because I admired their great knowledge and learned from them constantly. Anyway, she suddenly did not feel comfortable next to me anymore. Maybe she felt patronised, restricted, or whatever, it was never clearly communicated (like so much in Sri Lanka). Since she wanted to keep this job above all else, it was clear what her goal had to be: one of us had to go, namely, me. Who was more important for the functioning of the hotel? The intelligent woman knew that very well: she was. At the same time, Margrit and Wolfgang started to criticise me. Suddenly, I heard that I was not qualified to look after the guests psychologically. After all, I had no training in this field. My appearance was not professional. This and that happened and quite quickly I was pulled down from a pedestal they had put me on at the beginning. I no longer understood the world. They had invited me, had asked me to come. They knew me from before! They knew that I had given up everything to do this job. But now they didn't lift a finger to help me. Instead, I kept hearing comments like, 'You have to know for yourself if this is right for you.' The situation escalated when Dr. Ruvini announced she could no longer work with me, period. She refused to speak to me. That was only two months after she started work. Two months after I got her this job. Now the question was how our employers would judge the situation and who they needed more urgently: her or me!

CHAPTER 14:

He's Waiting Under a Palm Tree

In the hotel, camps began to form: was it for me or for Dr. Ruvini? It became apparent that I would be the loser and so they distanced themselves from me. Because, of course, nobody could afford to be against their employer. Even if one of the other employees perhaps secretly had sympathies for me, they were not allowed to show them. The Sri Lankans are very good at being neutral and stay out of such conflicts for self-protection. Understandable, because they did not want to lose their jobs under any circumstances. It was an enormously tense time for everyone, because the hotel area was small and we could not really avoid each other. Of course, I had to put on a happy face to the guests, because they were not supposed to notice anything of the crisis! It was not easy!

During this time of uncertainty, I was invited to a party: in mid-August, a friend invited me to her birthday gathering. It was just the right thing to do, to finally switch off for an evening, celebrate, have fun, get out of the tension at work. I was very happy. That evening I put on a beautiful dress and was driven to the house where my friend Miriam lived with her Sri Lankan husband. They lived in one of the typical one-storey bungalows with one bedroom and one living room, kitchen and bathroom. The property was surrounded by a wall, which was very pleasant as it protected us from the curious looks of the neighbours. As previously mentioned, Sri Lankans have no desire for privacy and like to be part of the life of their fellow Sri Lankans. We Europeans don't need that level of involvement and Miriam had been looking for this private property for a long time. They also had five dogs, and for this reason it was practical to have a wall. There was a garden of dusty earth with some grass and a few bushes and trees, perfect for humans and animals. The party took place outside, it was a wonderful tropical evening and I was in good company. I was beaming with joy, as I usually hung out in the Palm Villa staff bungalow in the evenings, where I would spend time with the other German guest attendant. She had also decided against me and for her job. Invited to the party were, as usual, only men. Friends of the husband, all of them around thirty, were sitting at several tables, on which the ubiquitous favourite drink was served: Arrak. Distilled from the juice of coconut palms, it is the most popular drink in Sri Lanka for any celebration: it is affordable and does its work quickly and safely. It is drunk with water or with soft drinks such as cola or lemonade. To soften the effects of the alcohol, there are various nibbles called bites. These can be boiled chickpeas with chili and coconut (my favourite), pieces of fish or chicken fried in oil and with onions and other vegetables or nuts - just little things to line the stomach for a long evening of drinking. Sri Lankan music is played, everybody sits and exchanges the latest gossip (very important) and becomes more and more cheerful and loud as the evening goes on. Usually somebody has a drum with them, and at advanced hours there is singing and dancing. The men come out of themselves, clad in shorts with naked upper bodies, and celebrate their brotherhood. Because that is what they call each other: Malli, brother. It took me a while to understand that this is not a name, because there were conspicuously many Mallis around me. Although I didn't understand Sinhala, I kept hearing Malli and everyone seemed to have the same name. I had to laugh out loud when Miriam told me that the word means brother! Local women were never present at parties like this one, at least not in the villages I visited. I'm sure it's different in Colombo. So, the men can let off steam and get drunk uninhibitedly because there are no disapproving female looks resting on them. So, besides the birthday girl, I was the only woman at this party. When I arrived, I noticed all eyes were immediately directed at me. But then the conversation continued in Sinhala (possibly about me) and I sat down with Miriam and congratulated her on her birthday. It was to be expected that I would only be able to talk to a few of the guests, because I had already discovered that not many of them spoke English. Sri Lanka was a British colony until 1949 and since then all children learn English at school. From the first to the last school day, every day. And unfortunately, only theoretically - because practically, they do not learn it at all. I will get into this subject later. But for now, the prophecy that the medium had made in Switzerland seemed to come true: my soulmate was waiting for me, palm trees all around us.

One of the party guests immediately caught my eye: while the other guys appeared in Bermuda shorts and t-shirts, he wore long dark pants and a white shirt with short sleeves. This made him look more mature than the others. Together with the dark skin, this made for a very appealing overall package. He was probably five and a half feet tall, so a little smaller than me, very slim with delicate fingers (I love slim hands). His well-groomed short haircut was chic, his black hair was wavy. His name: Chamara. It did not take long until he came over to me and introduced himself. To my great astonishment, he spoke a pleasant and fluent German. Since it was difficult to communicate with the other men, I enjoyed chatting with him and we sat down at a separate table. He was very polite, fetched food for me and filled my glass when it was empty. Charming, attractive, entertaining ... and obviously very interested in me. How much I enjoyed this attention after the last lonely weeks in Sri Lanka! I floated on cloud nine and danced exuberantly until I became a little unsteady on my feet after having enjoyed a lot of Arrak-Cola. We danced barefoot in the garden and I stumbled more and more over tree roots and holes that the dogs had dug there. It was time for me to go home and he offered to take me in his tuktuk. He had to leave now too. Not that he was sober, but in Sri Lanka they don't mind things like that too much. I said goodbye to my hostess and the other guests, Chamara started his red tuktuk and we clattered through the silence of the night. It was only a ten-minute drive until we were standing in front of my villa. The security guard, who protected the house and us ladies at night, opened the gate and I said goodbye to my new friend. He took advantage of the darkness of the hour and gave me a fleeting kiss on the neck ... and then I was inside the walls and he was on the way to his house. I probably shone like the moon and my heart was incredibly happy: I had not experienced such a beautiful evening for a long time. Of course, we had exchanged our telephone numbers and, as soon as I was in bed, a greeting came with good night wishes. Blissfully, I fell asleep and looked forward to what was yet to come. Was he my soulmate?

The next day, reality was waiting for me again. I had to go back to the Palm Villa, back to the hostilities and the feeling of not being welcome. In the afternoon another message from Chamara fortunately arrived: if I had time that evening, he would like to show me his hotel and invite me for dinner. When could he pick me up? Wow, the day suddenly looked completely different; of course I would love to join him. He also wrote that he had invited our hosts from the evening before, Miriam and Mohan too. So, there would be four of us. Yes, a definite yes! Time flew by and it was soon time to take a bath, put on a nice dress again, choose matching earrings and get ready in anticipation. In Sri Lanka it gets dark all year round at about 7:00 pm. This happens very fast because the country is so close to the equator. Within half an hour it is pitch black, especially in the village areas where there are few streetlamps. Charming Chamara came at 7:30 pm and looked as wonderful as he had at the party. I loved his mischievous smile and the dimples that appeared on his face. We stopped at the gate of a small hotel not far from the beach. After a short honking, an employee opened the door and we drove inside. At the gate, the name of the hotel was written in golden letters: Dolphin Villa. It looked fantastic, with its eight rooms on three floors. There was also a reception area, a kitchen, and an open restaurant. The rooms all had spacious balconies or terraces that faced the pool. The banisters and balcony furniture were made of dark glazed wood, had finely carved floral ornaments and offered a nice contrast to the white walls of the villa. The pool lighting was on and the bright blue made my soul sing. Jasmine and temple flowers bloomed in the garden and a few beautiful lamps emitted a mellow light. My heart was overflowing with joy. Chamara led me to the two tables that had been set up on the pool deck especially for the evening. Miriam and Mohan were already waiting there. Candles were burning in the glass cylinders and it already looked like a romantic evening. We talked about the party yesterday, which everybody had enjoyed. After a glass of Arrak, Chamara suggested a tour of his hotel. He beamed with pride. As there were no other guests there - it was off-season - I only saw a few employees who were watching us curiously. The other two already knew the hotel and so there was a guided tour just for me. Chamara told me that he had built the house by himself, that he had designed it and that he had raised the money all on his own. This is very rare in Sri Lanka, he said, because most of the locals have foreign donors who contribute financially and thus also become part owners of the property. Where did he get so much money from? He seemed to be a lucky child, because he had been to Europe several times before. At the age of fourteen, he had already started to earn money as a beach boy and thus got in contact with tourists. He must have been very likeable then, because soon he was invited to Switzerland and Germany. Thanks to a complete coverage of costs by his hosts and a written promise to put him back on the plane back to Sri Lanka, he got the necessary visas. Some Sri Lankans are never lucky enough to come to Europe, but he had hit the jackpot several times. And he had made good use of his time there: he picked up a bit of extra cash on the side doing various odd jobs for friends and family of his hosts. So, as he told me, he had been able to save money over the years to fulfil his dream: his own hotel. He taught himself

German and constantly improved it in contact with German speaking guests and on his travels. Through his visits he also knew the standard that Europeans want on their holidays and had built a house with spacious rooms and huge bathrooms. There were still one or two things he wanted to improve, but he had already come quite far. He had christened his hotel Dolphin Villa and had a large blue tiled dolphin mosaic laid at the bottom of the pool. I love dolphins, I love swimming pools, and I fell in love at first sight with this small boutique hotel as I strolled around barefoot. What beauty, what luxury! And then a man at my side, who I liked more and more.

Back at the pool, Chamara provided new drinks before he went to the kitchen to prepare our meal. He not only ran the hotel, but was also the chef. After his time as a beach boy, he had worked and gained experience in other hotel kitchens for many years. This is how it works in Sri Lanka: learning by doing. In addition to the welcome drinks, we had Roti, Indian flat bread, which we dipped in warm garlic butter. Very, very tasty and highly addictive! As the main course Chamara now served us grilled prawns (the big ones), also with plenty of garlic butter and delicious French fries. We all enjoyed this feast with a view of the pool and the starry sky, and I became happier and happier.

In the course of the conversation, I asked our host where he would be staying. He answered a little evasively: 'Sometimes here, sometimes there.' 'Here at the hotel?' I asked. Yes, if a room was available, he would sleep here. Or with his father, who was sick and needed help. He had to make sure he took his pills on time. That sounded very thoughtful. Another plus for him. Then Miriam threw in, 'Well, I guess you sleep with your wife sometimes too!' I froze. He wasn't married, was he? He hadn't given off that vibe at all - and I wasn't expecting it. More like, I'm single and I'm looking. Did I get that wrong? He quickly said that it was only on paper. He doesn't really have a wife, lives alone. He turned a little and quickly lit a new cigarette. 'What about your daughter?' Miriam asked. He had a daughter. I felt his heart was much more attached to her than to his wife. The daughter lived with her mother. And he explained to me that in Sri Lanka, divorce is allowed but it costs a lot of money. Moreover, the woman would then be without any financial security and would look like an outcast in society. He did not want that for his wife, he cared for her and the daughter, but they were no longer together, certainly not! My inner rigidity gradually dissolved, thanks to the Arrak and my deep wish that everything would be fine, and I was able to enjoy the evening again. We weren't a couple yet, it was all just a wish, a dream, a touch of infatuation. I decided to just be in the moment and relax.

CHAPTER 15:

Love Love Love

From that day on, I no longer felt lonely. Chamara sent text messages several times a day and seemed to be looking for a closer relationship. So was I. I accepted his invitation when he invited me to dinner at the hotel again. He would cook just for me. Oh yeah, I liked that. That evening I was freshly showered and dressed, and he came to pick me up. The hotel was empty again except for the staff who were hanging around somewhere. As young as Chamara looked at thirty-four, in his hotel he radiated an amazing authority and sent his boys to bring us drinks. They called him Bossa, the usual respectful form of address for a superior. We drank a Singha beer, reggae music playing in the background; it was another one of those wonderful tropical evenings I love so much. Fortunately, the mosquitoes don't like me very much, so I was mostly spared from their attacks in Sri Lanka. In the beginning, like every tourist, I had rubbed myself with citronella oil. But this smells too strong in concentrated doses and burns the skin like fire. And the locals survive without mosquito repellent. I lived here now, so I didn't put any more oil on, and it worked fine. Mostly, an incense stick was burning somewhere or there was a ceramic bowl under the table, in which a spiral of dried herbs (and poison) was burning: a so-called 'Mosquito-Coil.' Otherwise, like the Sri Lankans, at some point I developed a sixth sense of when a mosquito was sitting on my skin and batted it away. I never had problems in this respect, but I was always relaxed. With other foreigners I sometimes had the feeling that they attracted the mosquitoes just by their panic. Who knows, maybe the critters could smell our fear as much as dogs can.

That evening the food was again very tasty; there was rice and curry, the national dish in Sri Lanka. I had asked for chicken curry and red rice with a side of fried vegetables, and for dessert, fresh mango, my favourite fruit. Everything tasted excellent. Chamara showed me how to eat with my fingers, without a fork, and we had a lot of fun. After a short time, I got quite good portions in my mouth with my finger-fork - I didn't care how it looked. When Asians knead their favourite food into small packets, it always looks very easy and the mixture sticks together perfectly. Half of it trickled back onto my plate and the sauce ran in streams over my palm towards my arm. But all this didn't bother me at all, because the atmosphere was simply wonderful. Chamara was an entertaining companion and told many funny stories from his stays in Germany and Switzerland, and we laughed a lot. He could also tell all kinds of stories about the construction of the hotel, which had been going on for years. He had overcome many difficulties - but there were always new ones. The climate in Sri Lanka always demanded repairs, especially since the villa was so close to the sea. The salty air tore everything apart, even flowers – only a few thrive. Chamara had big plans for the coming season and wanted the Dolphin Villa to be in good shape again by December, that is in four months. He seemed to have everything under control. After dinner he suggested that we move to the balcony on the second floor and enjoy the view over the garden and the illuminated pool. Sure, why not! The balcony was a good sixteen square meters and had two typical brown wooden chairs, in which you half sit and half lie. The seats and backrests were woven. Our chairs were clearly a bit older and the seats were sagging quite a bit. So, we lounged and enjoyed the evening sky and the warm night. Slowly our hands found each other, armrest to armrest, and it got even warmer. Chamara was reserved and tender, not pushing me at all. At some point he came even closer and, as best he could in the armchairs, he looked for my mouth to kiss me. I kissed him back and it felt damn good. How long had it been since I kissed a man? Don't think now; it had been a long time. After a while, it became too difficult to embrace over the two armrests and we decided to shift to the canopy bed in the room. Well, what can I say, I was in seventh heaven! This was quite a big moment for me, because I had spent years keeping men away from me. It had been a full seven years since my husband had separated from me. Seven years of celibacy was clearly enough. I had a boyfriend again! So much could change so quickly. Chamara took me back to my villa and I continued to go to work the next few days, keeping quiet. But I didn't care much anymore. I was happy and up in the clouds.

In the meantime, I had hardly anything left to do as a guest attendant, because even the last tasks had been taken away from me. I was apparently no longer useful for anything and it became more and more clear that there was only one solution: I had to leave. But I had only just arrived! None of this made any sense! I had prepared myself for a few years in Sri Lanka; I had emigrated. Where should I go now? The jobs for foreigners are rare on the island, because even the locals don't have enough work. They were always looking for managers with experience, especially in tourism, but I had no training in this field. And working as a doctor in a hospital was out of the question for me. Not in Switzerland, and not in Sri Lanka either. Nevertheless, I searched the internet for jobs, both in hotel management and as a doctor, but I didn't find anything. A part of me was worried and helpless, because I knew that my money would not last long if I quit this job. But my heart was also full of joy, and in my infatuation, everything else was secondary. A solution would be found, I was sure of that. So, I did what had been hanging in the air for a long time and was inevitable: I sought out Margrit and quit my job at the Palm Villa. She seemed indifferent. No regrets, no lengthy conversation, it was simply noted. I, on the other hand, was very agitated and had to go to the beach and calm down. She wanted me to keep my notice period and so I had to be present for another two weeks, but you could no longer call it work. Afterwards, I was entitled to another fourteen days of vacation. Until then, I had to find a new job and also an apartment, because I had to move out of the employee villa. It was high time for me to become active! I had just taken the first step. The relief of escaping this tense situation outweighed my fears by far.

CHAPTER 16:

A Great Idea

The solution to my problems came from a direction I had never anticipated. Chamara once again invited me to his house. We always met only in his hotel, never in one of the restaurants on the beach. He listened to me sympathetically and said he was not surprised that Margrit and Wolfgang behaved so horribly. There were some stories about how they had gotten that coveted property right on the beach, and generally, they were not good people. Hardly any of the locals liked them. My decision to leave there was right, he said. And I shouldn't worry, he would take care of me. He said I was a great woman, I deserved help. And he had a proposal for me that would solve all my problems. I couldn't believe my ears. Could it be true? A new love, a new job and a place to live, all in one? And all this for me, who had been so unlucky? I was curious what that offer might be. Chamara explained: his hotel, the Dolphin Villa, had been built over a period of several years. Again and again, he'd had to travel to Europe to earn money there; he had already told me about this.

During this time, the building materials had repeatedly been damaged by the weather and some had been stolen. He only advanced slowly, the money was not enough, and he was playing catch-up. So, his former employer and long-time friend offered him a loan: he would lend him the money, but as collateral he wanted to have the land paper for the Dolphin Villa. I imagined something like a deed or the entry in the land registry. When the debts were paid off, the property would be transferred back to Chamara. Now it was time to renovate the house again and he needed money and management support. His hotel was not yet registered on online platforms like Booking.com and Tripadvisor, his website was outdated, the internet connection was not stable. He needed a new computer and a new telephone line to the hotel. It would be great if I could take care of the marketing, but I could also stay here for free. At the moment, he had a few bookings from guests who had already been in the area and met him. After he had shown them around his cute villa, they had booked rooms with him for the next season. He had all this in his head, not many yet, but it was a start. We could be successful together. Next season, we would then be fully involved. All we needed was a little money. Did I have that? Phew, that knocked me out. I could have a hotel in the land of my dreams, near the beach, with a pool, with the man I loved. I would enjoy the work and although I was not an internet specialist, I could learn. The only question was where to get the money I needed?

My bank account was at an absolute low ebb for years. I was combing my brain for possibilities. and I found what I was looking for. There was a possibility! Yes, that was it, I was rich after all. When I quit my job, my employer asked me where he should transfer the money from my pension fund to. This is the so-called second pillar of pension insurance in Switzerland, into which both employers and employees pay. If you change jobs, the accumulated assets go into the pension fund of the new employer. Over the years, this accumulates a nice sum of money, which is paid out as a pension when you retire, in addition to the Old Age and Survivor's Insurance, an obligatory form of national insurance in Switzerland. Since I could not specify a new employer, I had my money transferred to the vested benefits account of a Swiss bank. According to the law, it was blocked there until I retired - or until the time I applied for payment. After some online research, I came across the following words: permissible reasons for releasing the money were the acquisition of property, i.e. a house or apartment, or the financing of an existence abroad. There it was! I had money, and not just a little bit! There were several tens of thousands of francs in my account. And I could have it paid out to buy a hotel in Sri Lanka. What a lucky coincidence! I was on fire and told Chamara about my idea. He was of course also enthusiastic and urged me to complete the formalities quickly so that we would be ready to renovate before the season started at Christmas. Now it was already the end of August. I found out which applications I had to make where and within a few weeks I had the entirety of the pension fund in my account at the Commercial Bank in Galle. This was exciting! I had never had so much money at my disposal before, I felt really blessed by luck. I was rich, now everything was possible!

CHAPTER 17:

The Adventure Begins

On a Tuesday, the time had come for us to fetch the money from the bank. Mondays were always so crowded, so we chose to go on a Tuesday; I remember it perfectly. Chamara picked me up in his tuktuk and off we went. I stood in the long queue of people who wanted to be served at the counter. Meanwhile Chamara sat on the couch in the waiting area. He kept a constant eye on me, and I felt wonderfully protected. I filled out the slip the clerk gave me and was asked to wait a moment. After only ten minutes I was called again. In front of the man were piles of Sri Lankan money: it was several million rupees. He piled them up in a paper bag and handed them to me over the counter. This happened in front of all the other waiting people and employees, as if I had bought a t-shirt. I left the counter and Chamara was at my side. Together we went to the tuktuk and drove off. When I think about it today, I can hardly believe that we were not robbed after we left the bank. Was I scared? Did I have doubts? A large part of my pension was in my lap and I was about to leave it to a man

I had known for five weeks. There was not a hint of doubt. Even though I had received two phone calls in the last few weeks from well-meaning people who had warned me. Both a Sri Lankan and a German tried to dissuade me from my plan. They claimed Chamara was not to be trusted. They told me to stay away from the hotel and the man. I had hardly listened to them and said that I already knew what I was doing and had almost forgotten their warnings by now. There was a lot of envy in Sri Lanka, I knew that, and I had put these calls out of my mind, consumed with love for this man. On this Tuesday I was very calm, serene, full of trust, completely fixated on Chamara, the self-made man who had fought his way up. The man who knew how things were going in this country that was still foreign to me. The man I loved. I wasn't afraid. And my head was empty. Only later did I hear the expression that was coined for European women who come to Sri Lanka and invest their money there: They leave their brains on the plane. Yes, it could have been like that. I was certainly following other tracks than the tracks of reason. It was a big decision, one that had much deeper causes than the obvious ones. And one that would have consequences far greater than I could have imagined.

On that fateful Tuesday we brought the paper bag with the millions of rupees to the Dolphin Villa and Chamara put it in the safe. He wore the key on a chain around his neck. I can't remember if we celebrated that day, but I don't think so. It was kind of no big deal, it was normal. For me it was logical: Chamara needed money, I had some. Of course, I gave it to him. That's how I was. I was happy to help, and I would get something in return. My future in Sri Lanka seemed secure. I remember that we went to a shop in the afternoon with some banknotes and bought some paint. White wall paint for the facade as well as sandpaper and some means to work on the wooden railings on the balconies. These were our first issues. The wood suffered most from the humid sea air and everything had to be thoroughly cleaned and re-stained. Fully packed, we returned to the hotel and were welcomed with cheers. Well, they were actually not that loud. Sri Lankans don't tend to be loud in expressing their feelings, unless they've been drinking. But the staff at least looked very happy, helped immediately to unload the shopping and took care of me. The next day, craftsmen came to the hotel, painting and sanding. It was time for me to move to the Dolphin Villa to join in. It was now my new home and also my professional future. I had a hotel in Sri Lanka. How great it was! An exciting future had just begun.

My notice period was finally over and I was allowed to leave the Palm Villa. The last afternoon I was graciously released, I was allowed to leave after lunch. I had bought a cake for the local employees; I had gotten along well with them. It was a reason to celebrate: I was starting a new chapter in my life. On the part of the owners there was no fuss, business as usual. As a farewell, Margrit pointed out that my visa and residence permit were linked to my job. Since I had two weeks of vacation left, the employment contract ended after this time, just like my visa. She advised me, now apparently concerned about my wellbeing, not to seek illegal ways to stay in the country, as it would surely be discovered. I can still see the scene in front of me: Margrit was standing on a raised porch looking down on me, I was standing on the lawn below her. Very symbolic, because that's the way she had treated me in the last few weeks: from above. She was probably as happy that I was leaving as I was. Why, I still don't know. I had no idea how to solve the problem with the visa, but first, I had only one goal: get out of the poisoned atmosphere of this hotel from which I had been so brutally bullied. Let's go! Chamara came to me in the staff quarters and we loaded my possessions in two suitcases. The gates of the Dolphin Villa opened wide as we arrived, and the staff took my luggage to room number two on the first floor. I now had a luxury room with a king-size bed and a gigantic balcony with pool view. I had a new home and was simply happy. And yet, the sheets on my bed were old and torn, and did not fit on the mattress. And there was not a single flower in the room as a welcome greeting, I noticed immediately. I was a little disappointed. In the Ayurveda hotels where I had been to retreats, I was always welcomed by a wonderful profusion of flowers and towels. Well, I guess there hadn't been time. No big deal, there were more important things!

The next day I fully slipped into my new role as hotel owner. Not that we had drawn up any papers, a contract, or an agreement. It was an unwritten agreement that I was now part of this hotel and I attributed a role to myself. Besides the Bossa, there was a group that I always called the boys: they were not boys, of course, but grown men. In the rural area where I now lived, everyone always wore Bermuda shorts, t-shirts and flip-flops. And one decisive characteristic made them seem like young boys to me: that they were always together as a group. It reminded me of school classes. In Sri Lanka it is common to have physical contact with your friends, to hug and hold hands - separated by gender, of course. I often saw the boys sitting very close together, giggling like little children. It is quite normal to work together and to meet privately, to live together, and have this close contact. This is the case in many countries with a warm climate, but definitely not in Germany or Switzerland. For me it was a very unusual sight in the beginning. I think this closeness has an important social function in a country like this, because it strengthens the bonds between people. And for women, it also has a protective function. Alone, they are not safe; sexual assaults on women are unfortunately frequent. For women and men alike, it is definitely true that it is better to go through thick and thin together, and in Sri Lanka it is often quite thick and one is glad about any support from one's mallis, brothers or sisters. I often envied them for this solidarity. Such closeness was foreign to me and I probably could not have lived like that. Nevertheless, it looked like security and I missed it.

So, our boys were a cook, Chaminda; an assistant cook, Ruvan; a housekeeper, Sampath; and an all-rounder called Rasta. Rasta helped where it was needed, ran errands, cleaned the pool and tended the garden. He drove the laundry to the cleaners or guests to the next temple. The boss did ... yeah ... hm ... so, the boss was mostly on the road, or so he told me when I asked him where he was. 'I'm on my way, honey.' It could be anywhere. For example, he went to the fish market or had to do something important, organise, discuss, shop. I didn't see him very often, really. But he always kept the reins in his hands and ordered craftsmen for the woodwork and bought paints, rollers, brushes, and everything else that was needed for the renovation. He assigned the task of painting the walls to the boys. They had no experience in this, but they had time, and why should we pay more people if they already got wages and bread? So the four of them set to work and began to paint the walls in the first guest room. Always in a good mood, at a leisurely pace and constantly chatting or singing, a happy community of good friends.

I, on the other hand, familiarised myself with the computer. In the meantime, we had a new telephone line, which should ensure a better internet connection. I registered the Dolphin Villa with Tripadvisor, Booking.com and Lonely Planet, a travel guide in book form that gives recommendations for hotels and restaurants that are particularly worth visiting. Together with Chamara, I redesigned the website. We gave the rooms fancy names like Superior Bedroom and Luxury Bedroom, depending on the floor they were on. We redefined the prices - higher of course - because we would soon be able to present everything much more beautifully and that had more enjoyment value. I translated the website into German and slowly I had the feeling that I was running a hotel. There were booking requests, which I always had to discuss with Chamara, because he still had the old bookings in his head, which had to match. He absolutely didn't want to write them down, for whatever reason. Furthermore, he got calls from beach boys who needed a room with their ladies for a night or just a few hours. The only time I heard about this was when they came to see me in the hallway or in the restaurant. That gave a little extra income - for Chamara. He remained the boss. The work on the computer I could only do step by step; I had to work a lot on my own, because I had no idea about these things.

Aggravating to my inexperience was the fact that the internet in Sri Lanka was very susceptible to interference, no matter which line we had. In rain, wind, or thunderstorms one could not work at all. And as it was monsoon season, there was plenty of all of those things. We were always on guard during a thunderstorm that could start from nowhere, unplugging the power plug so that our precious computer was not ruined by a lightning strike. My mental capacities were exhausted at some point during the day, so I looked for other activities that were physical and independent of the weather. There was a lot of other things to do and I wanted company. Often, I heard the boys talking and laughing in Sinhala and felt very lonely. There were no guests in the hotel, and I didn't really have any friends. I hadn't seen the friend who introduced me to Chamara since the night after her party. I wanted to be part of the boys' community and decided to help with the renovation. I quickly saw where there was a need: like everywhere else in the world (I think) the boys had started work without planning ahead. (I apologise to all the men who do this!) Our troop had happily started painting, but without any covering to make sure that the paint didn't end up on the tiled floor. And once it had dried there, it was very, very, very difficult to get it off again. Yes, and I chose this difficult task for myself. Of course, I made sure that they covered the floor in the following rooms first, but it was not enough. There was a lot of paint to be removed and I, the madam, sat on the floor and scrubbed the tiles. That was exhausting, especially considering that we had about 30 degrees heat and the air was always humid - tropical. Air conditioners were only in a few rooms and they ate a lot of electricity. When we had no guests, they were switched off. Electricity was very expensive in Sri Lanka, especially near the beach where we were. The tariff was higher there than in the countryside. I was always sweaty and after two hours of scrubbing I had limp arms. But I had company and, hey, this was my hotel! Who doesn't know the stories of the emigrants who start new lives in foreign countries? It costs sweat and tears, we know that, and I was willing to give that. The sweat, I mean; the tears are another story ...

CHAPTER 18:

Shopping

The first big purchase that had to be made was not furniture, but a visa for me. I had no idea how I could get a new resident visa to legitimise my stay in the coming months. A tourist visa would not be enough, as it was only valid for four weeks. How should I solve the problem? Of course, Chamara knew: 'Honey, it's not a problem, I'll take care of it!' I had to give him my passport, and within a week I had a brand-new visa with a stamp and everything for a whole year. It looked just like the old one. Magic! I didn't ask any questions, just happy that the burden was off my shoulders. It probably wasn't quite legal, but who cared?! With the necessary change, everything seemed to work. I did not care; the main thing was that I could stay in Sri Lanka now. Then we started with the actual shopping: it was more than clear that we needed new sheets and towels, new pillows (they mildew terribly fast in this climate because they attract the humidity), things for the restaurant like tablecloths and place settings, ashtrays and candlesticks. For the kitchen many things were missing like good knives and also dishes. I'm sure there was more we had to get, I don't remember exactly, because everything was not very structured. Just now, I remembered TV sets and a satellite dish. No, it went completely different than at home, different than I was used to, and different than I expected. I was looking forward to our shopping trip like crazy. First, I love shopping. I love to furnish and decorate rooms. I love colours and I now had my own hotel and wanted our guests to feel comfortable in it. Second, Chamara and I would go shopping together. That was special because I saw him so rarely. He was actually married and told me that that was why we couldn't go out together. He never slept at my place, but left around 10 pm to go … wherever. To his father or his mother, who lived separately. Or his wife - I never knew for sure. We actually only ever spent one single night together in our hotel and I didn't really get the feeling that he enjoyed it. Chamara was always very restless, couldn't sit still, wiggled his legs and was always talking on the phone. In Sinhala, of course. I could sit next to him and listen and yet I didn't know what he was saying. Then he suddenly had to leave again and didn't come back. Cigarettes were with him wherever he walked and stood. He was always on the go somehow, always on the move. I learned to tell whether he was in the hotel by the flip-flops in the entrance area or by his tuktuk. Sometimes he was there, but I didn't see him, because he was in a room and had closed the door. He did not greet me. If I saw his tuktuk but not him, I would ask one of the boys if the boss was there. Sometimes I'd hear, 'Yes, madam, he's sleeping.' I'd find him in an empty guest room, fast asleep with his phone beside him. I wasn't happy with this behaviour, but I thought it corresponded to the mentality of the culture. Men do their thing and women are left out. He was the boss. And me? I continued to fight my way through the lonely days and waited eagerly for the little pieces of attention and time together. How frugal I was!

Our shopping expedition was therefore a highlight for me. We started with the pillows. I got into Chamara's tuktuk and he drove us to a dealer who made pillows with a coconut fibre filling. They negotiated in Sinhala and I was allowed to choose between two different thicknesses. Then we bought twenty of them and stuffed the plastic-wrapped cushions on the back seat and in the small shelf behind it. I had the task to prevent the slippery packages from sliding around, because otherwise they would have inevitably ended up on the street. I sat on the hardback seat and could have used a good eight arms to keep them all in place. Thus loaded, we arrived at the Dolphin Villa and were welcomed by the happy boys. So now we had cushions, a start. We would not be able to buy many other things nearby. Chamara knew two big shops in Colombo; we would get everything there. 'When do we start?' I must have asked five or six times. 'Maybe tomorrow, honey, I'll let you know.' I was looking forward to the next day. Chamara wasn't. Tomorrow, then. Then it rained, then his daughter had something important to do at school ... or the wife was sick and had to see a doctor. There were always reasons not to go and I was really annoyed - and disappointed. I knew that some things were really important to him and required his presence. But I felt really stupid, because for me the shopping trip was the most important thing.

Then finally everything seemed to fit and the ideal day for our shopping trip came. Chamara had gotten a minibus and a friend to drive it, because he himself had no driving licence. In the morning at breakfast, I was still sceptical and held back my anticipation in case of another postponement. But then both Chamara and his buddy came, and it really started happening! My excitement rose, the joy dared to show up shyly and I dressed up for the city (I didn't want to look like a country bumpkin, after all). So, sandals instead of flip-flops! Chamara opened the back door of the minibus for me and I got in. When I sat down, the sliding door behind me closed and he went to the passenger door. He sat down in the front next to his friend. UGH!!! I was alone again! This was not at all how I had imagined it. I said in German, 'Chamara, why are you sitting in front? I want you to sit with me!' He responded, 'No, honey, I can't do that, the driver would be alone. I'll sit in front, why don't you stretch out in the back and enjoy the journey?' I was close to tears. Damn culture, damn habits, damn country! I knew that mallis always stick together. But I was also important, and I didn't want to be alone! I wished for nothing more than for my darling to be near me. At least on that day when we spent my money on our hotel. I was sad, angry, frustrated, lonely, disappointed. I didn't even want to go anymore, I didn't care, I didn't give a damn! All my joy was gone, I felt once again not understood and not taken seriously. We drove off anyway, lively chatting in the front, silence in the back. Until Colombo, it was the usual long drive and we drifted with the familiar stream of tuktuks, buses, cars, bicycles, pedestrians, cows, dogs, and so on, slowly towards the capital. I sulked to myself. Now and then Chamara asked me if I was okay and I answered briefly. Finally, we reached the city and went to the first shop.

The Odel was the Mecca of all foreigners and wealthy locals: here you could find everything, from clothing to jewellery, small furniture, decorative items, bed linen and towels and also a supermarket for special culinary needs (cheese, dark bread and many other delicacies). A kind of department store, as you would see on every corner in Switzerland or Germany, but a rarity in Sri Lanka. My eyes could hardly take it all in. I had been there before and bought clothes, because there was a lot for the taste of us Europeans - and also our sizes! Sometimes, I had trouble getting something in size 40 in smaller shops and cotton was not easy to get. The Sri Lankan women are smaller and more delicate than me and have a different taste in fashion: ruffles, sequins, Hello Kitty, pink and even synthetics are popular. It dries faster in the tropical humid air and is non-wrinkle, which is certainly an advantage. I did not like it at all. So now we could dive into the huge offerings and the variety of the big shop and I breathed a sigh of relief. Beautiful music accompanied us; it was clean, it was a luxury temple. My senses danced, my heart dared to open up again a little. I wanted to enjoy this now, so swallowed my anger and went with it. The shopping went quite smoothly; Chamara was at my side and the driver trotted after me. I finally had the feeling that we both were on the road as a couple and had a common goal. There were some nice things we both liked, and we filled our shopping cart. Chamara paid cash and we loaded everything into our bus. Afterwards we drove to Barefoot, also a magnet for all foreigners. There were many fabrics, pillows and blankets made of natural materials, many hand-woven and all in the brightest colours. I loved this place! There were many other handcrafted things like wooden Buddhas, jewellery, bags, sarongs and other seductions. Oh, I would have loved to buy everything, but the prices were a bit steep. So, we just bought some table runners for our restaurant and nice candlesticks and with that we had everything we were looking for. All this excitement for three hours of shopping! I was happy, but somehow the bitter aftertaste of disappointment remained. After a stop for a quick lunch of rice and curry, we went back to our hotel, taking the same route as on the outward journey. The big day was over, and I returned to the daily routine of cleaning and internet. The paradise didn't feel so magical anymore …

One evening, I was alone in my room and the boys were somewhere chatting. There was a knock on my door: 'Madam, come downstairs, towels.' I didn't understand what it was about, so I was curious to know what was waiting for me. I found a small van standing under one of the garden lanterns and Chamara talking to the driver. 'Hi, honey, we need new towels. Take your pick.' The back of the truck was full of towels and sheets, each stacked in clear plastic. There were different colours, qualities and sizes. It was a pitch-black night, and the lantern lamp was sparkling. A groping in the dark, searching through the piles to find the treasures within. And the whole situation as joyless and trivial as buying a pack of cigarettes. Since we needed a lot of laundry, it would cost us a lot of money. I would have liked to have made this purchase under different conditions. Somewhere nice. Well, so it was again different than I expected, but it was certainly cheaper than elsewhere. The purchase was made quickly, and I was released into the evening again.

CHAPTER 19:
Variety

It really wasn't easy for me to find a fun leisure activity to balance my work. There were many foreigners who were so attracted by life in Sri Lanka that they bought a house there or rented it on a long-term basis. They either lived there permanently or came regularly for the winter months to keep warm. Many spent their days drinking and smoking together (at least, that's how it looked to me). Over time, I knew some Germans and Englishmen by sight and knew that it always got quite loud near them. This way was never mine: I'm not a party type, I don't like alcohol and I don't enjoy this sort of party setting. I love music, especially outside and preferably in the evening at the beach. I like reggae, I like to dance barefoot, and I also like to laugh. But I'm more of a quiet type and feel more comfortable in a small, familiar group. I can enjoy silence and the beauty of nature. So, I never felt the need to join the party people. Near Galle there were some tourist places where you could listen to music in the evening. I especially liked Unawatuna, a bay that firstly offered calm water for swimming, and secondly, many guesthouses and restaurants right on the beach. I remembered this from my time in the Hotel Svedana. In the high season, between December and April, it was very loud here in the evenings, as many parties were going on. During the rest of the time, in the restaurants, one also heard music playing in the background, but the sound did not fill the whole bay. When I felt like a change, I liked to ride my bike to Unawatuna, grab a couch, and spend some hours on the beach - it was like a holiday. Or I even went to one of the expensive hotels nearby, where as a visitor I could use the pool and the beautiful garden for a small fee. One vacationer among many. I love beauty, I love luxury, and these little breaks gave me the feeling that I really lived in paradise. I could not spend much money, because my savings slowly melted away: I had no income since my work at the Palm Villa ended. And all of my money was in the safe! My wallet was running low. Incredible when I think about it today: I didn't even ask Chamara to give me money to have fun. I didn't have any at my disposal, yet there were millions of rupees in the hotel safe! I had given him all my money and had let go of it. It was exclusively intended for the renovation of the Dolphin Villa.

So, I looked for low-cost ventures to enjoy. The choice was small. Walks on the beach sound nice, but during the day it was often too hot for that. It was also not a pure relaxation because I was often hit on by the eager beach boys who wanted to sell something or were looking for company. In our area most of them slowly got to know me and left me alone, but at the beginning it was really unpleasant. There are no cinemas, no museums, no footpaths inland (unless I walked on the small paths, where the wild dogs also liked to walk). Swimming at other beaches was also an idea, but in many places, there were such strong currents that it was dangerous. Whether it is safe to swim in the sea there depends crucially on the season: in the months of the monsoon season, it is stormier, and the sea is choppy. On the southwest coast of Sri Lanka, the rainy season is from May to September, on the northeast coast from October to April. It's funny that there are such differences on such a small island, but it's true. If you are planning a longer trip and want to surf or sail, it is worthwhile to plan well in advance with regard to the weather. Although this is changing more and more; the conditions are not as predictable as before. In the area where I lived, the sea was often too turbulent for swimming. But even when it was calm and clear I could not bring myself to go snorkelling alone. Even though I'm a water lover, I was afraid. So, I was left with swimming in hotel pools (of course, in our own) and hanging out on the beach of Unawatuna. I am not usually so dependent, but in Sri Lanka it is really no fun to be alone as a woman. At least that's what I think. Even when the beach boys knew me in the nearer surroundings and did not expect any money from me, the locals were always very sociable. Then I had no quiet minutes, I attracted them like moths to a flame. Be it in the bus, on the beach, wherever. I seldom felt like interacting, because it often went in the sexual direction and at some point, it tipped from a happy mood into the Leave me alone mood, which could escalate further to Fuck off! Yes, I began to discover this side of me: I learned to say clearly and distinctly, no. At least in the small things of everyday life. That was the learning experience of it, which was good in the long run, but the afternoon was always ruined afterwards.

From time to time I was invited to parties that took place in the families of our boys. There were many parties, because in

Sri Lanka people like to celebrate for a number of occasions, not only on religious holidays. The following events are celebrated in a big way: weddings (these are actually two celebrations in one), big girl parties, and funerals. Birthdays are also celebrated with pleasure, albeit on a smaller scale, and I was certainly invited to these most often. As described above, the separation between men and women was always predetermined, whether the families were Muslim or Buddhist. This was part of the tradition. Only men were invited to the men's birthday parties, but I was invited as the guest of honour, so to speak - or perhaps because people hoped I would bring a bottle of Arrak. Both were possible. I didn't go so often because I didn't like it. I had no children, no husband, so there was not much to talk about with the women in the family, if communication was possible at all because of the language barrier. Often the women were so shy that a collective giggle was the only thing I encountered. They were usually not to be seen at all. Then I felt uncomfortable, also because I didn't understand what they said about me among themselves in Sinhala. But the biggest challenges for me were the personal invitations: 'Madam, my family would like to meet you. Come to my house for dinner!' At first, I was flattered and liked going. Then, as time went on, I became less enthusiastic and tried to apologise. I noticed that the evening always went like this: I was picked up from the hotel. Before that, I had bought a present for the guest, which I handed over. No flowers, that was too cheap, because flowers grow everywhere in Sri Lanka, like coconuts. A cake was more popular, or dishes or glasses, something a family with many people and guests could use. Once I took photos of the family during the invitation and afterwards had prints made in a photo shop. That was a great gift in retrospect, because most of them didn't have a camera and today's smartphones were not so common there yet. So, for the first time, the family got a photo that united them all, something very valuable. I had it laminated so it could survive in the humid air for a long time. It was placed behind glass in the living room buffet and is probably still there today. The present was handed over, then I sat in the circle of the family, i.e. with the parents, grandparents, siblings, children and grandchildren in a place of honour, and was interviewed: how many children I had, where my husband was, where my family was (the parents) and whether I liked Sri Lanka. This was answered quickly, and it was then up to me to ask how old the children are and ... then what? Most of them had no job, never had one, there were no hobbies, I didn't know the TV soaps myself, so every subject was quickly exhausted. Then, of course, there was the wedding album to marvel at, even the parents' album, if the inviting person was not yet married. Afterwards I made a few compliments and jokes and after an hour I was already exhausted. In the meantime, I had drunk two glasses of sticky fruit juice from a carton and could not possibly manage a third. With great relief I heard the question: 'Are you hungry?' Which I answered immediately with 'Yes!' Then I was invited to the dining table, where numerous bowls of rice and curry dishes were waiting for me. All under newspaper, so that the flies did not walk on them. I was allowed to sit down, and all the others disappeared, at least to the next room through the door, from where they watched me eating. (The doors were actually just frames in which cloths hung; there were few doors that could really be closed. This way the air could circulate better.) A woman stayed close by, always scooping food onto my plate and asking me if it tasted good. I found this part of the program the most difficult, because I was alone again, but was also observed! With luck I sometimes managed to have the head of the family and the son, who had invited me, to eat with me. That was much better. The food itself was delicious and I was always very touched by how much effort the women had made. And I do not want to appear ungrateful, I really do not. There was certainly not chicken for the family every day, but they had prepared one for me. I love curry, which every family prepares according to their secret recipes, and I also like spicy food. So the food itself was the highlight of the evening. But such occasions were not cosy and relaxed. After I had eaten, the women and children ate too, but in the kitchen or outside, I never saw them eating. Soon after, it was acceptable to say that I wanted to go home. Of course, it was my own fault that I still did not speak Sinhala, so every conversation was difficult. But honestly, we didn't have much in the way of conversation to exchange either. We lived in the same village but in two different worlds.

CHAPTER 20:

Meetings and Musings

Meanwhile, I had been living in the Dolphin Villa for two months and the renovation work was nearing completion. We had painted all walls including the facade, and the rooms now had air conditioning. The old appliances had been replaced because they were completely rusty. All rooms now also had a flat screen and on top of the hotel was the satellite dish. It was pretty much useless, because we could only tune in to three channels and our guests complained all the time. Not having a TV would have been more honest. The restaurant had been decorated with beautiful murals, in the style of the famous Sri Lankan artist, Bevis Bawa, who has inspired the decoration of many hotels in the area. Bawa's former residence is near Aluthgama and is now known as Briefgarden, a popular destination for tourists in this area. It is a beautiful property where you can see the house as well as many paintings and sculptures by the artist. He and his brother Geoffrey are very well known in Sri Lanka; they were successful architects, artists, and bon vivants around whom many stories are entwined. I didn't really like the mural – it was painted with black paint on the white wall and looked very morbid to me. Plants are only black when they are dead. But that is the Bawa style that is revered in Sri Lanka. The Bossa prevailed here. The guest rooms were allowed to be more colourful. Chamara and I agreed that the rooms in our hotel would get a personal touch. Our guests should remember the Dolphin Villa after their return and be happy to come back. So, my friend had collected photos and newspaper clippings of shells, tropical fish and sea animals and asked a painter friend to paint them directly on the walls of the rooms. I was allowed to choose which motifs I liked best, and beautiful frescoes in pastel shades were created. Perhaps they are still to be seen today.

One day we were together in Galle at the fish market when Chamara suddenly greeted an older woman he knew. She spoke Swiss German and came from Bern; her name was Rita. After exchanging the usual pleasantries, he invited her to join us for a tea and she happily agreed. Somehow, she seemed surprised by his frankness, and she looked at me questioningly. Two days later she came by when the boss was on the road again. She had phoned Chamara in the morning and agreed to come to our hotel at 2 pm. Since our mutual friend was late, we first had time to talk. And it was a very interesting conversation. I learned that Rita had been the one who had invited Chamara to Switzerland several times many years ago. She had thus opened many doors for him and had also given him the opportunity to earn money to build his hotel. She was in her late sixties, twenty-five years older than Chamara, and it remained unspoken what kind of relationship they'd had. At some point, they had somehow fallen out and lost contact (no comment on this from either side). She herself had been coming to Sri Lanka every year for ages, just like me. She spent the wet and cold winter months there because she thought it was good for her rheumatism. But this was not the only reason for her stay, it was only half the truth: she was in the middle of a court case, and had been for years. Rita, like many foreign women, had become involved with a lover in Sri Lanka with whom she had built a house. She had always been a hardworking and very sociable woman and had worked at all levels to get her little guesthouse up and running. Her numerous friends came and spent the holidays with her, and they brought new guests with them. It went well. Rita cooked and cleaned, and her boyfriend was active where he could be. He also helped in the kitchen, learned to cook from her and much more. It could have been so lovely, but it ended in a fiasco. Rita could be very quick-tempered (I could feel this already that afternoon), she was much older than her boyfriend, and had certainly worn the trousers in the relationship. The way she sat in front of me at that time, I could vividly imagine how she had led the command. In dealing with the probably sensitive and not very self-confident Sri Lankan man, she might not always find the right tone and the necessary patience. Anyway, one day she shouted at him when he left something too long in the pan in the kitchen again and that was the breaking point. He'd had enough of the criticism, enough of her, enough of the whole situation. He grabbed a long knife and went at her with it. I guess it got pretty serious. A guest intervened and prevented worse from happening. She fled from the home she had built and financed. He told her that he would kill her if she came anywhere near the property. Strong stuff! It had been five years since that horrible experience. For four years she had been trying to get her property back, or even part of the money she had invested. There was a court case going on and she had already spent vast sums of money on lawyers. They wanted to be paid in advance for each trial and the whole process went on and on and on. She had been in the courtroom in person several times before. The trial was in Sinhala and she paid for an interpreter, yet she did not understand what was going on there. Her request was repeatedly postponed, she kept paying money to keep everything going. She was in the right and she wanted her money back. But the prospects were bad, everyone told her that. And there were many people who knew about the subject, because it was a well-known one. Rita also knew many similar cases and still couldn't stop trying. Because what annoyed her was, of course, on the one hand that she had lost her money and her house that she had built for old age. With her Swiss pension, she had wanted to live comfortably in Sri Lanka without paying the rent and the high living costs she now had at home. But on the other hand, and perhaps even more, she was angry about the physical attack on her. Even though he had not physically hurt her, she still carried an emotional wound that would not heal. And her medicine was called justice. She was looking for it and she would not give up! The crowning glory of the whole drama was that her ex didn't even live in the building! The former guesthouse fell into disrepair and was ransacked, the garden was overgrown. A sad picture. I felt how Rita was eaten up by this destructive fire of her feelings. She had hardly any money left for daily expenses, not even in Sri Lanka, and went to Switzerland to work as a cleaner, to afford the travel and the trial. I felt very sorry for her. Her story was not the first and not the last I heard. I met a woman who built two houses over the years for two men to whom she was married under Sri Lankan law. It happened exactly the same way both times, as if there was a script for such cases: when the house was finished and the last door was inserted, it was closed in her face. From inside, by her husband, who was inside with his local wife and children - and stayed. He had already been married when she married him. Somehow this is possible in Sri Lanka. This woman, an English woman, is still on the island; she just can't get away from this country, just like Rita.

While we were drinking tea, the two of us came to talk about the Dolphin Villa. She told me that Chamara had a girlfriend before me who had supported him financially during the construction phase; she was probably Russian. She still threatened him by phone and email because he owed her money. I froze inside, but the message didn't quite reach me this time either. I had put on an insulating layer that didn't really allow such information to reach me. Yes, it could be that Chamara had cheated on the Russian woman, but that was not my story. That was someone else's story. Rita noticed my short moment of uncertainty and made optimistic remarks: Chamara had spoken so positively of me when she talked to him on the phone. I was sure he was serious about me and the hotel looked beautiful how we had renovated it together! We ended the conversation with small talk, and she rode her bike back to her modest rental apartment. Unfortunately, the boss had not managed to come. Of course, the conversation had an effect. My subconscious was running at full speed. What was going on? What would happen next? I had understood by now that there were many complicated relationships between the vulnerable tourist women who visited Sri Lanka and the local men. They started with a physical relationship and felt like genuine love for the women. These women were mostly only single, some divorced, all in their forties and older, not so much in demand on the dating scene. I could well understand how they felt, because I was exactly in this age group. The relationship began very easily and playfully, bringing the woman the sense of appreciation and fulfilment she didn't find back home. She felt wanted, she had value again, she had fun. She blossomed and in no time the holiday flirtation turned into a serious relationship; Sri Lankan men do not give up quickly. The men fought with all their strength to bind their sweetheart to them, because they all dreamed of a better life, maybe even a life in Europe. Many vacationers considered buying a house in Sri Lanka, where they could come on vacation and move after their retirement, just as Rita had planned. But not only single women had the desire to spend their retirement in the tropics. Many foreigners dreamed of a life in the warmth and the demand for land was great. But the Sri Lankan government had put a few limitations on the sale of their paradise. One of them was a law that allowed foreigners to buy land in their own name, but only by paying an astronomical tax. I think it was 100 percent of the purchase price, which is an enormous amount. To get around this, land was bought in the name of the local boyfriend or beach boy who had arranged the purchase. The Sri Lankan promised fervently that the buyer would have no problems with the deal but would certainly save a lot of money. The second part of the promise was true. He promised the woman that he would always love her and that he would always take care of her, especially in old age, and that it would of course be best to buy the land in his name to avoid paying taxes. The lovelorn woman would believe this only too gladly. From there, the story could go a few different ways. I got to know some of these ways in the following time.

They rarely went well - for the woman, I mean. But after Rita's visit, I still did not see all this so clearly. Not yet. But my mistrust had been fuelled by Rita's stories.

I didn't know any more stories at that time, but I didn't have many opportunities to talk to other women either, because I was given a chaperone. Suddenly one day Chamara offered that his good friend Kumara would drive me with the tuktuk everywhere I wanted to go. I shouldn't ride a bike anymore – it was just too dangerous. And the heat! In the beginning I liked the idea; I could make longer trips and I was not alone. The catch was that Kumara spoke almost no English and appeared to not understand my attempts at communication. But he was persistent: he did not let me out of his sight for a second. This soon annoyed me, and I began to feel that instead of giving me more freedom to go on excursions, it was restricting me. I didn't understand what this was all about, but I avoided calling him more and more often, and soon simply refused to ride with him. I explained this to Chamara emphatically and he just said succinctly, 'You know best, honey.' In theory, I was free again. But Kumara continued to annoy me because he was omnipresent. As I said before, I did not always know when Chamara was in the hotel and when he wasn't. He didn't spend much time with me. There were always more important things. But for Kumara he apparently always had time. He appeared every morning and had something to talk about with Chamara behind closed doors - or to do? I couldn't figure it out and I was jealous. What were they doing there every morning? I asked Chamara and he said vaguely, yes, it was because of the land paper, there was so much to organise, and something had to be rewritten and he always sent Kumara with orders, copying and so on. Hm, okay, what should I think and say to that. It had to be so. Nevertheless, Kumara never became my friend, I kept my distance from him. And brooded.

Finally, there was a change: we had guests at the Dolphin Villa. A mother and daughter from Tel Aviv booked a double room for one week. They didn't have much money and Chamara did them a special price. They were also allowed to get things from the supermarket to eat in the restaurant to save money. Both were very open-minded and funny, and the boys enjoyed them. During the day, they took the tuktuk around and visited Buddhist temples, the fort in Galle, breeding stations for sea turtles, or other beaches. Our cook Chaminda drove them where they wanted to go. He spoke English best of all of the boys and had an obvious crush on the daughter, who might have been in her midtwenties. Anyway, they stuck together all the time and he used all his charms on her. In the evening, we met in the otherwise empty restaurant: Chamara, Chaminda, the two ladies, and me. They had brought a water pipe from Israel and, for the first time in my life, I smoked a sheesha with apple-tobacco. It tasted wonderful and I loved it when the pipe made the rounds. And I also loved that Chamara finally spent evenings at the hotel and we spent time together: we played cards; I can't remember what game it was. I was quickly introduced and joined in, although I always lost. The others, on the other hand, played an ambitious game. I soon noticed how incredible Chamara's memory was: he knew exactly which cards had already been played and which could still come. He often won and seemed very much in his element. I noticed and admired him: he was apparently quite clever. I was proud of him. Every evening after dinner, the same group met and there was a game of cards. It was a welcome change; finally, I had fun again! The week flew by and already it was time for a farewell evening with a special dinner. Chamara spoiled us with his cooking skills and we played cards one last time. After a few glasses of Arrak, I said goodbye and went to my room. Shortly after that I heard the bed squeaking in the room above me, and other noises also indicated that Chaminda's efforts were crowned with success in the end: he spent the night with the beautiful woman from Israel. His wife was expecting their third child and I suppose he wasn't allowed into her bed. Anyway, it was none of my business. Then the ladies were gone again, and the nice evenings were over for all of us. These evenings left me with a mixture of memories, and one detail of them in particular had a special meaning, as I understood much later.

One evening, after Chamara had said goodbye to me, a light suddenly came on in my head: I realised that he always had remarkably wide pupils. His eyes were also always reddened, but I saw that in many Sri Lankans. I traced it back to the infections they all went through again and again. When the monsoon season starts and it is humid and cold for a long time, the people there drop like flies. Everyone coughs, has a fever, and has to take medication. They are just so used to the heat, and the damp and cold weather makes them sick. I thought to myself that the red and sometimes yellowish discoloured eyes were the result of all these infections. It looked like a liver strain and Chamara liked to drink. But his pupils were dilated? Suddenly I froze: was he taking drugs? I had never tried anything but alcohol and had no experience in this area. But suddenly this subject came into my consciousness and scared me. I sent him a text message and asked him if he was taking drugs. He replied briefly, 'What kind of drugs?" That was the end of the subject for him, and I didn't follow up. I was still that gullible. Or rather: the repression of painful truths still worked. I had no more questions for him; I had imagined something. No need to worry! Nevertheless, the topic came up again after a few days. When I chewed on it in the evening, I wanted to talk about it with someone. I went downstairs where Susanta, our night watchman, was watching television. I knew he had known Chamara since high school and asked him if he was taking drugs. Susanta answered evasively, concluding, 'He's a good man!' What did that mean? I wasn't any smarter than before and knew that it wouldn't be worthwhile to keep on drilling. It was going to be a long, slow while before I understood more.

CHAPTER 21:

There Will Be a Wedding

The Dolphin Villa was really an eye-catcher, with the freshly renovated building, the blooming garden and the pool. Therefore, naturally it came about that it was also booked for wedding celebrations. In Sri Lanka, a separate branch of tourism has developed to fulfil the wish of many bridal couples to experience an unforgettable ceremony on a paradise beach. Our villa offered the ideal setting for this and was booked by foreign as well as local guests from time to time. Of course, we also offered this on our new website. For the foreigners, there was a kind of all-inclusive package with which they got accommodation and food for the bridal couple and possible guests as well as the social program. This included: makeup and hair for the bride, transport of the bridal couple to the beach with a decorated tuktuk or buffalo wagon, and a welcome by traditional Kandy dancers in magnificent costumes accompanied by local musicians. Then the wedding ceremony on the beach under a flower-decorated arch (if the wind allowed it), champagne to toast, and a wedding cake.

The whole fairy tale was then crowned by a ride on an elephant for the bridal couple. This moment always included a lot of laughter, because ascent and descent were not so easy, especially for the bride in her beautiful dress. The whole ceremony was captured by a photographer and the couple received a photo album to commemorate this special event, also included in the price. Such offers exist at many hotels in Sri Lanka and the photos are a decoration for every hotel website. Many women's hearts beat faster at this performance and it can be very romantic to celebrate your marriage vows barefoot in a flowy dress on the beach. However, these marriages are not legally valid; there must be a marriage ceremony at home by a registrar. I vividly remember a special wedding at the Dolphin Villa: a Russian couple had rented the whole villa and brought friends and family. They were partly accommodated in other hotels, as was I, because my room was needed. I had nothing to do and nothing to say that day, everything was under the direction of Chamara, who had his boys firmly under control and his eyes everywhere. I was present during the ceremony, which was really beautiful. The weather was perfect and the part on the beach was very festive. After the wedding ceremony, everybody came back to the Dolphin Villa, and after some ceremonial drink rounds, there was a barbeque under the starry sky and fireworks. The atmosphere was marvellous, and vodka was flowing in streams, despite the steep price. The Russians had stocked up well in the duty-free shop at the airport. I went away early to my alternative hotel, because Russian weddings are not my thing. I couldn't join the party and had nothing to do, so I felt kind of out of place. When the wedding party had left after three days, we would clean for days and also partly repaint the walls again. And collect broken glass from the pool. It had gotten pretty crazy. Russian guests are coming more and more to Sri Lanka, and while they are stereotyped as being a bit challenging and rowdy, I've found them to be really pleasant. But sometimes you do need strong nerves and not all hotel owners are happy about the wishes of the wealthy but also demanding guests. I hadn't joined the party, but I took something important away with me: I now knew why Chamara's eyes had caught my attention. He was smoking marijuana! When I asked him about it, he just laughed and said, 'Honey, this is not a drug! I have been smoking it for twenty years and I am not addicted. Do you want to try it?' Now, finally, something was clear: one of the many questions was answered. Fortunately, it was not a harder drug. Wanna try it? Sure, I wanted to. We smoked a few times together after that, and I liked it, but I was fine without it. Was he?

In addition to requests for foreign wedding ceremonies, there were also requests for domestic ones. Weddings are huge events in Sri Lanka, and 200 guests and more are often welcome. This is very different from what happens in Europe and I found it interesting to get to know another important part of the culture. I was able to take part a few times. The two families are in debt to celebrate this once in a liftetime event with great splendour. It is the highlight of their lives. There are two celebrations: the actual wedding day is hosted by the bride's family and takes place either at the bride's parents' house, in a hotel, or in a restaurant. The bride wears a white sari, and the groom is often dressed in traditional clothes (I don't have the words to describe them) or alternatively wears a suit of western style. Often, there is a waistcoat and I can imagine that it is quite warm wearing it. But the bride wears several layers of clothing, because the saris are made of solid fabric and cover the body in many layers. Most of the time, as far as I have seen, the bride and groom are sitting, serious and sweating in their thick clothes, on a red velvet couch. There are many photos taken and the guests deliver their congratulations and gifts. This couch will be delivered to the hotel of their choice together with an artificial flower bow – it must be important. At the end of the celebration, the woman leaves her birthplace and things can get very melancholy. Her family must let her go now. The newlyweds then go on their honeymoon, which usually lasts only two days. They spend this time in a hotel room; often, family members stay nearby. Afterwards, there is a second party at the groom's house (and at the groom's expense): the homecoming is celebrated. Here, the colour red dominates, both in the bride's dress and in the decorations. After the party, the bride moves to her new home, to her husband and his family. Before the marriage, the woman lived sheltered with her parents and often she met her groom through a marriage broker. They usually see each other only a few times before the wedding and never alone, so they hardly know each other when they make their marriage vows. The trust in the validity of the horoscopes as well as in the wisdom of the parents is so great that this decision is respected. It is the tradition. However, there are now more and more couples who get to know each other spontaneously and decide for themselves who they want to marry. So, during the two short honeymoon days, the newlyweds get to know each other a little and explore each other sexually. The thought of the latter awakens an immense resistance in me, and I hope that this custom is now outdated. The two hardly know each other and have to start a sexual relationship that evening on command. They are tired and anxious and therefore this marriage begins with stress and possibly physical pain. It is still quite common for the family to be nearby on the wedding night (perhaps even in the next room) and to check the sheets after the bridal night: did the bride really enter the marriage as a virgin? After this act and the days spent together in a hotel, homecoming is celebrated, and the couple returns home to the groom's house. In the future, there will hardly be any togetherness anymore, because the couple will be part of a new extended family. I have heard that it is now quite common to celebrate both parties on the same day and to share the costs. After all, it is also a question of money.

The Dolphin Villa was to host another wedding after the Russians' celebration. A distant cousin of Chamara wanted to have her homecoming party there. I heard about it two days before the event when I noticed how busy everyone was suddenly. They bought tons of food, cleaned up the garden and brought huge pots to cook rice and curry for 150 people. It was a smaller gathering by local standards. Once again, I was left out, because I had no idea what was going on and what I could do. As madam, I could not possibly cut vegetables or scrub pots with the staff - it was not allowed, as it did not correspond to my position or whatever. In any case, I was not allowed to help when I offered it. I would have liked to join in, because then I would have had something useful to do on the one hand, but on the other hand I wanted to be involved in what was going on. I had no chance. 'Go to the beach, madam,' the boys gave me some friendly advice. I'd been doing that almost every afternoon now. I took my cigarettes and a book and sat down in a restaurant on the beach for an hour or two. I had started smoking because Chamara was smoking and the cigarettes were now a kind of companion for me. I didn't really like it, but there were circumstances that were even less pleasant. I was unhappy and lonely, and I had almost no money left to do anything. And my thoughts circled incessantly around the subject of what else? What was to happen next: did I have a future at the Dolphin Villa? Did the relationship with Chamara have a future? Somehow everything had gotten out of hand. It was high time to act, although I had no idea how. Where would I go? What would I live on? That evening before the wedding celebration, in which I was again not included, suddenly I'd had enough: enough of humiliations and disappointments, enough of lies, enough of the unbearable loneliness. I had to act and take a first step, although I did not know the second one yet.

CHAPTER 22:

A Step Into the Unknown and How an Angel Catches Me

My decision was suddenly crystal clear: I was leaving Chamara! Finally, I was ready. I started packing my things the night before the wedding. Until deep into the night, I sorted out what I would take with me and what I could do without. I still only had my two suitcases to fill, that was all I could take with me. Books, some clothes, trinkets and souvenirs had to stay there. I smoked, I drank Arrak, I cried. No one noticed. Nobody cared. I planned to go east the next day with the departing guests. For once, we had two young Norwegian men as guests who were on a road trip in a minibus. Following a spontaneous idea, I had asked them in the evening if they would take me for a ride. But I did not know where to go yet. No problem, was the answer. I had finished packing my things in the morning before the wedding party, had breakfast just like the guests, my boring toast with omelette and the fruit plate, although I had knots in my stomach and was struggling with tears. The men paid their room bill for the four nights in cash and I took the money. It was the only cash I had at my disposal. When their driver came, I asked one of the boys to get my luggage down. 'Where are you going, madam?' 'I am leaving - I'm leaving!' Consternation on the faces around me. 'But the Boss ain't here, Madam!' That's just fine, I thought, and got on the bus. At that very moment, Chamara came barging through the gate and looked at me in disbelief. 'Where are you going, honey?' I declared, 'I'm leaving you, I've had enough!' I felt incredibly tired and sad and hurt. But at the same time, totally sure that this was the right step. And I enjoyed the horror on his face. Oh yes, a small, bitter triumph, but so infinitely soothing. Then the sliding door closed, and we drove off. When we were on the main road, I said to the two Norwegians, 'I just left my lover and my job, I'm free!' And I took a deep, deep breath! The two of them nodded. I'd broken free from an unhealthy relationship and had come back down to Earth. The question was, where to now? Maybe that's the whole point of my not having left before. I didn't know where to find shelter, because I had no friends to take me in. And I didn't have the money for a hotel. The Norwegians wanted to drive further along the coast and stay somewhere where they could party. Their destination was as open as mine. I started to think about where to get off, because I had no desire to join them in partying. I needed a place to calm down and sort out what had happened in the past three months. Yes, really, only three months had passed since I had moved into the Dolphin Villa! For the life of me, I couldn't think of anything. I saw the places in front of me through which we would travel and sifted my memory for possibilities. Suddenly everything had to happen so fast! Did I know any people somewhere who would take me in my stricken situation, anywhere I could find comfort? Finally, it occurred to me that I had already been to this area to do an Ayurveda program. The Sea Turtle Beach Hotel was near Weligama, about thirty kilometres northeast of Galle. I had the feeling and hope that this hotel could give me refuge for a few days. It seemed to me like an island of security in all the uncertainty and darkness and I asked the driver to stop there. At the entrance, I said I was looking for a room and wanted to talk to the German hostess. She came immediately - it was a woman I did not know - and asked how she could help me. I had trouble describing my desperate situation, but I was able to make her understand that I was in need and was looking for cheap accommodation. Since I had been to this hotel before and it was also off season, I hoped for a special price. With a resident visa I could hope for an additional discount. Somehow, I would be able to pay it and after that I would surely see more clearly how to continue. The extremely compassionate woman promised to talk to the management and disappeared. I fell into one of the thick chairs and prayed for help. After only ten minutes, she was back. Her face already expressed what she had to tell me: unfortunately, there was no special price for me. She was really sorry. I felt nothing but emptiness and was unable to say or decide anything. I was just about to fight my way back up and go to the bus when she said she had an idea. She wanted to help me. She reached out her hand to me and said, 'By the way, my name is Angela.' Angela, an angel, stood before me, a sign from heaven! I have a close relationship with angels, and they have often comforted me and helped me. My heart took a leap. What came now? I sat down again and listened to her proposal with curiosity: she had rented a small house nearby with a friend. This woman was in Germany for two weeks and her room was empty. She was certain that I would be allowed to use this room and find temporary shelter there. She suggested that I let the driver drop me off right now. In the meantime, she would ask her friend by text message if it was okay with her. I was completely floored and unspeakably relieved and of course gladly agreed. This angel had grasped my distress and offered me the perfect solution. She was really a helper from heaven. After only a ten-minute drive, we reached the rented house and I said goodbye to the two Norwegian angels who had taken me along until then. Totally exhausted, I sank down on Angela's couch and hoped for some good news. I would wait there to find out if I was allowed to stay. For this I had to switch on my mobile phone again and saw that Chamara had called several times, wanting to know where I was! I was still happy that he had been so surprised by my moving out. After about an hour, Angela called me and told me that I was allowed to use the room. She had reached her friend in Germany and she had no objections. Hurray, I had found a shelter! I could rest, sleep, cry, think, and plan. The relief was enormous, my gratitude boundless. I threw myself on the bed in my new room and fell asleep.

Angela did not come home every evening, because she had to stay some nights at the hotel where she worked. So, I had a lot of time for myself - actually a little too much, because I was in a dark hole. My mind was searching for answers, but I couldn't ask anybody. After a few days, I picked up the phone when Chamara called, but I didn't tell him where I was. He asked when I was coming back, and I said never. When he knew that I was still in Sri Lanka he called less often, but every two days he threw out the bait again. I said I wanted to talk to him, he said yes, when I came back home we would talk. There it was again, the word home. Home - where the fuck is home? That was my big issue: if I had known somewhere in Europe where I felt at home, I would probably have gone back there. But there was no such place. During my childhood, we moved so often that I didn't feel at home anywhere. I did not want to go back to Switzerland, from which I had emigrated seven months ago. There was no sense of home in Switzerland or Germany. And even if I went back, where to? I had no strength for a new beginning, no money and no idea. And I still couldn't believe that my big dream to live in Sri Lanka had burst so easily and my money had disappeared. I could not let go yet; the wound was too big. And I still had hope for a happy ending. I thought that I could surely still somehow pull the wheel around and at least get my money back. My time with Angela was limited, as her roommate would be back soon. Again, it was time to make a decision. And I decided: first of all, I would go back to the Dolphin Villa, talk to Chamara and find answers. And, most importantly, I would settle the matter of money. That was crucial. Maybe it hadn't reached the bottom of the sea, lost forever. Maybe it was still floating somewhere, and I could retrieve it. I called him and the next day a car came to pick me up and drove me back to the Dolphin Villa.

'Welcome home!' he shouted from the first-floor balcony as we drove onto the property. Chamara was beaming. The boys were also happy and were eager to carry my luggage to my old room and bring me something to drink. It was about 6 pm and Chamara had only a short moment to give me a kiss. Then he had to go to the kitchen to cook. It was the end of November and three rooms were occupied. At 7 pm, I also went to the restaurant and was served with a relieved grin from him. But his attention was completely focused on the guests. After the meal, they had questions about excursions, and he sat down at their table with a glass of beer. There was nothing I could do, and I understood that this was important now and could not wait. So instead, I waited in my room. We had agreed that he would come to me later to talk. I was agitated, wondering how best to approach my topics, and waited. It was 9 pm, 10 pm ... he didn't come. I tried to see from my balcony where he was, but I couldn't find him. I texted him, and he replied, 'I'll be right back, honey.' I was smoking cigarettes, and I was smoking inside, in rage. That asshole! And I fell for him again. I hated him, I hated myself, I hated Sri Lanka! He came around 11 pm, we were both tired and postponed the conversation until the next day. I hated myself even more. Of course, nothing happened the next day or the day after that. We never really talked – I mean in such a way that I would have gotten more clarity. I had to come to terms with it, what was left for me. I now knew for sure that I had to leave Sri Lanka and I thought about where I could go. Where was my new home? And what else could I do to save my money?

The decision about where I would live was closely related to the possibility to earn money. Although I had studied medicine and had a basic training in general medicine, I had not really worked in the field for about twenty years - except for the last two years, when I had worked as a consultant for a Swiss health insurance company. I was also a qualified homeopath and had worked with it for many years, but I didn't want to be self-employed anymore. And where were there that employed homeopaths? I could only think of clinics that dealt with holistic medicine. But I didn't like the idea of integrating myself into the daily routine of a clinic at all. After I had enjoyed so much freedom of movement, I didn't want to be caught in a web of guidelines and restrictions, even if it meant a regular income. But actually, I had lost my interest in homeopathy. This direction no longer felt appropriate. So, I listened to myself, and thought about how it would be to return to the health insurance company in Switzerland. There I'd had very nice colleagues and had been bid farewell with great regret. I could easily imagine returning there, so I wrote an email to ask if they had a vacancy at the moment. And, oh wonderful miracle, they had! They were happy to see me again and I was able to sign a new employment contract. I wanted to work full time, but at first, I only agreed to a limited period of nine months. I wanted to return to Sri Lanka for the winter, in October. This story was not finished yet, I could not easily finish with my dreams and my feelings. My farewell would not be completely final. My employer got involved and I breathed a sigh of relief: it was easier than I thought! Happiness was finally on my side! Then came the question of accommodation; before, I had commuted from Lucerne to Zurich, which meant a daily commute of ninety minutes each way. Now I was happy to be closer. I didn't have any furniture anymore and needed a shared room or a furnished studio. And again, a miracle happened, as if by magic. A colleague at work had a friend who lived in Geneva. He had a one-room apartment in Zurich, which he rarely used and also rented out temporarily. And the best part was it was located in the exact district where my company was located, namely in Zurich-Wiedikon. Ten minutes' walk to work, that was perfect! I rented it for nine months and had thus laid the foundations for my stay in Europe: I had a job and an apartment; I could travel back soon.

Now I had only one thing left to do in Sri Lanka: I wanted to document that I had lent money to Chamara. Because I wanted my money back. If not now, then surely in a few years. I wrote a letter in which I stated that I had lent Chamara money for the renovation of his hotel and that he committed himself to pay it back with interest over ten years. I found a notary in Galle and showed him my document. He said it was all correct and we arranged an appointment to sign it. I was still living in the Dolphin Villa and was waiting for Chamara to come and pick me up at the time. But he didn't: I received a call from him that he was there at the notary now and that I should come! Asshole again! So, I got on my bike and went over. There we both signed the contract and a huge burden fell from my heart. I had been incredibly naive, but it was going to be alright. I was sure of it. Now I could finally leave. I booked a flight to Hamburg to celebrate Christmas with my family. On the 28th of December 2010, only eight months after my emigration, I returned to Europe. I had experienced so much, it felt more like eight years.

CHAPTER 23:

Welcome Back

I spent the Christmas holidays with my parents, my siblings and their families. They were all very compassionate, which was balm to my soul. I didn't tell them everything in detail, but they didn't ask, and I was fine with that. I was not proud of my experiences in Sri Lanka and felt like a failure. With what high expectations I had moved out and how everything had gone! After a week in Hamburg and time to adapt to the cold weather and European time zone I flew to Zurich on December 30th. My new home was in the attic of an old apartment building in Zurich-Wiedikon. It had pitched roofs, and it was tiny, with a kitchenette and a shower room. And it was inexpensive. It was perfect for my needs. I could open the windows wide and enjoy the beautiful view over the roofs of Zurich and into the vastness of the sky. The commute work was short; I could even have gone home for lunch. Most of the time, I went for a walk during my breaks, because eight hours of work in front of a computer is a challenge for a person born in Gemini: I need exercise, fresh air, variety. I had to get this during my breaks or after work. The stupid thing was, of course, that I was new again in Zurich, so I hardly knew anyone. There were a few work colleagues there, but they were not really friends. So, I explored the city on my own. I like Zurich; the city centre is small, and with the bus or the tram I got everywhere fast. I especially loved going out in the evenings, something I had missed so much in Sri Lanka. Finally, I could be on the road again without danger, and could go out alone at night; it was very liberating. Especially where there was so much to experience! The city is located where the Limmat flows out from Lake Zurich, and there are many nice bathing possibilities and sweet cafes. My favourite destination in the summer became the women's bath, where during the day only women are allowed to bathe. It is a bathing establishment that is as old as its name sounds. It consists of a wooden house perched on the river, with a screened bathing area, and can be reached from the shore via a wooden jetty. This bathing establishment is lovingly maintained and looks very cute from the outside. In the interior, there is a kind of basin that is formed by wooden planks. Thus, one swims in the fresh river water and is still protected from boats and the current - a dream! Of course, there are snacks and a bar, so that women can really enjoy themselves during the day. I loved lying there on the wood and letting the waves rock me when ships passed by. In summer, barefoot discos were held there, which means that on Saturday evening from 8 pm, guests of both sexes were welcome to dance without shoes. And when the weather was good and you could see the stars above you and the beautiful Grossmünster and Frauenkirche churches next to you, I didn't want to be anywhere else!

Of course, there were also many lonely hours in Zurich, but

my heart was not quite there either. My thoughts often went to Sri Lanka. I had not yet finished, neither with the longing for Sri Lanka, nor with the relationship to Chamara. In May, I became very restless: my fiftieth birthday in June was approaching and I couldn't stand being in Switzerland anymore. I wanted to spend my birthday in the country of my heart. So, I booked a flight, and thanks to holiday and overtime, I could travel to Sri Lanka for four weeks. I was quite exhausted from all the work, including night and weekend work, and my emotional processes, and felt ready for an Ayurvedic retreat. Fortunately, I had earned well and could afford it. I booked a retreat on the south-west coast, near Aluthgama, which is a good distance north of Galle. I would have a healthy distance from the two hotels where I had such painful experiences. I could hardly wait to finally be back in Sri Lanka.

CHAPTER 24:

I Celebrate Myself

When I look back today, I can hardly believe that I went back again. All I know is that I couldn't help myself back then. For many years, I had dreamed of living in Sri Lanka and I could not just turn off this longing. It was not Chamara who had drawn me there. It was other things that had been calling my soul again and again for years. I often thought about what attracted me so much to this country. Again and again, I had discussions with other emigrants about it. Because everyone, really everyone, experiences great difficulties and obstacles and more than once finds themselves about to travel back to their home country. They find themselves at the point of burying their dream in order to save their soul and/or money. Because it is always about existential, deep, touching, great things. Sri Lanka offers the perfect setting for drama. But after a lot of whining and wounds, almost all emigrants stay and it is always the same things that keep them: the climate, the light, the colours, the beaches, the rice fields, the water buffalo, the lotus flowers, spices, people, the slowness of being ... often it is a mixture of everything. But also, the highlands with their green tea plantations and vegetable fields with more mild weather touches the heart. As well as the experience that we can live comfortably with little possessions. With much less than we were used to. Personally, I have always been drawn here by something else in particular: the glow in people's eyes. Many Sri Lankans are poor as churchmice, many are out of work, losing their few possessions again and again through floods or storms. But they have this special glow in their eyes. They have a healthy pride, get up again and again, build up their houses and go on. I see this glow in their eyes. How can that be? Where does it come from? Maybe because they are less brainwashed than we are and live more from the heart. I don't know. They're very emotional and they can be very dramatic; I've seen that a lot. But I think they have a basic trust that it will always continue, somehow. That's their experience. There is no health insurance, no unemployment benefits, very few people get pensions. But they live in the moment, from one day to the next. They celebrate their festivals, borrow money for them and somehow or other perhaps pay it back at some point - or not. They pray to Buddha (or Christ, Allah, or the Hindu gods) and are firmly embedded in the calendar of their religious festivals. And they are firmly connected with their families, neighbours and friends in a way that we experienced in Europe perhaps 100 years ago, and which is rare today. I wanted to forget the disadvantages of this closeness for a moment ... I missed this glow in the eyes of the people – it wasn't to be found in a rich country with social security, full supermarkets and big cars. I missed it painfully. In Sri Lanka I often heard: 'Madam very nice, always smiling'. That's how I am, most of the time, and I am sometimes tired of smiling into the void in Europe. In Sri Lanka, I got a smile back. The locals also seem to notice the missing glow in the eyes of my fellow countrymen: even if they spend their holidays in a luxury resort, they are rather serious. They do not smile so freely, so openly. They are often anxious and insecure. Perhaps they are afraid of losing some of the many things they own. Money is a serious thing.

But I finally wanted to have fun again - and relax. These were my declared goals for the holiday. So: off to Sri Lanka! When the sliding doors in Colombo airport opened and I stepped out into the tropical air, tears came to my eyes: I was home again, I was happy! The Ayubowan Reef Hotel, which I had chosen for this stay, was located directly on the beach of Beruwela and offered an unimpeded view of the Indian Ocean. In addition, there were wonderful bathing possibilities due to the offshore reef, which held off the dangerous currents. This reminded me of the Hotel Svedana where I had been years ago. It also had a large saltwater pool, so that I could really swim in any weather - as I said before, I love pools and that was half the holiday fun for me! In a previous life I was probably a mermaid ... I had a beautiful room with a terrace facing the sea, and gratefully let myself fall into the routine of treatments. I already knew the procedures from other retreats and could immediately switch off and enjoy. I quickly found a few women with whom I could chat at meals or on the beach, but in between I also enjoyed the peace and quiet, alone. There was a lot to digest on all levels. I started to think about how I wanted to celebrate my fiftieth birthday.

But before that there was another birthday in the calendar: my angel Angela also turned fifty and she wanted to celebrate this occasion in a proper way. I think the round birthdays are really something special. Angela, who had welcomed me so kindly a few months ago, had been living in Sri Lanka for several years and had a few friends here. She wanted to enjoy a meal with all of us, to dance and have fun. Therefore, she rented a small beach restaurant and invited us there at the end of May. I was in the middle of my retreat and actually detoxifying, but I thought that fun was also important medicine, so I wanted to make an exception for it. Only for one evening out of the monastery! I also wanted to see my soul sister again; we had become very close during our time together. So, I told the hotel that I would not be back before midnight and rented a car with driver (which is very affordable in Sri Lanka and highly recommended). At about 6 pm I was picked up and we drove off, heading south. After a two-hour drive we reached the beach restaurant and met many Sri Lankan men, some foreigners of both sexes, and Angela in a party mood. She had dressed up specially for this evening, wearing a long colourful dress and a flower in her hair. The DJ played typical Sri Lankan music, in which the word adare, love was the main part. This is the favourite musical theme there; it is like the corazón with the Mexicans. Everything revolves around love, all over the world. When I arrived, everyone was already standing or sitting with Arrak, beer or gin, and the typical bites. To celebrate the day, I had bought a Black Forest cherry cake at the German bakery in Aluthgama. Angela laughed out loud when I handed it to her and even more when she read the creamy inscription: Happy bday Angie. That was a successful surprise - a greeting from the old home country. But before the cake fight, we danced the best we could and smoked the best we could. Besides the local cigarettes, there was also ganja and I thought it was time for me to smoke a joint again. I have a rather low tolerance for alcohol or other intoxicants, but I wanted to give it a try. It was a wonderful party, within minutes the clothes stuck to our bodies and our hair was plastered to our heads. Who cared?! The light warm wind from the sea and a few fans helped to cool us down again. And more drinks of course! There was a delicious buffet with rice and curry; everybody was happy, myself included. Around 10 pm it was time for me to return to my hotel. I had kept an eye on the fact that my driver drank little alcohol and now I had to trust that he was really fit to drive. As soon as I sat in the car, I fell asleep in the back seat and woke up in front of the Ayubowan Reef Hotel. I found it hilarious to sneak into my room smelling of alcohol and smoke, and giggled softly. My personal cocktail of renunciation and excess was brilliant after all. Life was one big party!

The next morning, things looked a little different: I had to get up early again. I had already cancelled yoga, but the rest of the day's program was fixed and immovable. The therapists had their plans and breakfast was soon over. So, time to get out of the mosquito net! Arriving at the treatment cabin, I was pampered and cared for as usual, which fitted perfectly to aid my deep relaxation. Then came the part with the needles: acupuncture. This was part of the program here. I had never been a fan of it before, but I had noticed that it did me good. Well, most of the time – but perhaps not after a night of partying. At the same time as four or five other spa guests, I was to receive my daily ration of acupuncture healing. In the treatment room there was no talking, only peace and quiet. I lay down on my cot and the poking began. Ouch, ouch, uhhhh...ohhhh, I simply couldn't go on! I am already mega sensitive without weed and alcohol in my system but with - no thanks. After I had emitted some inescapable noises of pain, I asked to stop with this treatment for the day. Tomorrow I should be sober again (I said quietly to myself). 'I am very sensitive today, very fragile,' I said to the doctor. She nodded sympathetically. And then I set about cleansing my body of the poisons of the night before. Crazy, yes, it had been unreasonable to go out and party, but I wanted to be a bit wild! Nearly fifty and still not too old to celebrate!

There were only ten days left until my own birthday. What was I going to do? On a deck chair overlooking the ocean, I started planning. I had few friends to invite. Apart from Angela and the boys I'd known at the Dolphin Villa, I knew of no one. Chamara was of course not an option. I hadn't quite let him go yet, but I certainly wouldn't invite him. The boys had always treated me respectfully and they would bring a good atmosphere, so I decided to invite them. However, I had a very special idea: I didn't want it to become a pure gentlemen's evening again, I wanted to invite them together with their wives. That meant then, also with their children. Because only three of the men were married and had small children, it would not be a huge group. But something different for my local friends. For the party I also chose a beach restaurant, this time near the Dolphin Villa, namely in Talpe, south of Galle. Close by is the Hotel Svedana, and the area was still familiar to me. After finishing my retreat, I moved to a guesthouse in Unawatuna, in my favourite bathing bay. I found the perfect setting to celebrate my big birthday. Restaurant and food were reserved, friends were invited, there was nothing more to do. Then there was only the important question which of my colourful cotton dresses I should wear, and which earrings should dance with me into a new decade of life. Both were quickly decided, and since I had lost two kilos again during the retreat (despite the party feast), I really liked my short dress, with tanned skin and sun-bleached hair. A sexy single woman, ready for new adventures! Angela came to me on the morning of my birthday. We spent a wonderful day in and around the Indian Ocean, had prawns and a cocktail at noon, and did what girls do: enjoy. Freshly showered and dressed up, a tuktuk brought us to the party location in the evening and soon the others arrived on their bikes and in tuktuks. I received touching gifts: they had put a lot of thought into making me happy. I received a Sri Lankan shirt with an elephant on it, wonderful incense sticks and a big package with fine Ceylon tea from the highlands. In addition, a handmade card with the message, Happy Birthday, Madam. Even a photo of me was glued on, a printout from the internet. I was deeply touched. Then the party really started with the drinking and the bites, and soon the boys and also we two girls were pretty tipsy. Despite our coaxing, the wives didn't drink a drop of alcohol and preferred to sit at a separate table. They were busy with the children, who soon got their food and then fell asleep on their mothers' laps. The men took off their t-shirts, the landlord brought his drum, and then there was the singing and dancing I loved so much. I noticed that it was actually not a good idea to invite the women: neither did they look happy, nor could the men really let loose and enjoy the party. They were now under supervision and I noticed how they were holding back. Yes, well, I could not change the habits of the people and I learned to accept them. But I had at least tried to integrate the women for one evening. Maybe they enjoyed it after all. Everything was fine, I relaxed, and we had a nice evening. Of course, at some point it ended, because the women slowly nodded off and the men had to bring their families home. It was a special evening that I will never forget. I was now fifty years old and I decided that a new phase of my life should begin, in which I was happy and had a loving partner by my side. Wishes can come true. I deserved it! At least I was already in the land of my dreams. The rest could still come, and I was ready!

CHAPTER 25:

The Next Chapter

But first, it was back to Switzerland for me, because my employment contract ran until the end of September - and it was only June. I had four more months of full throttle work, then I wanted to go back to my island and find happiness. I moved back to my small rooftop apartment in Zurich and was glad that summer had also arrived on this side of the globe. I wanted to celebrate my fiftieth birthday with my family, and I flew quickly to Hamburg for a long weekend. Luckily this did not cost the world, as it is not a long distance. The time in Europe flew by and, as is usually the case, after half of the time it flew by faster, at supersonic speed. I was able to store my few belongings with a friend in their basement and before I knew it, I was already back at Zurich airport, boarding for Sri Lanka. I love all airports and I always loved the moment when it was time to travel again after all the work, packing and planning. What was I planning to do in the land of my dreams and nightmares? I had no clear plan. That is, I had one, but it left a lot of room for manoeuvre: I still wanted to live in Sri Lanka. That automatically meant that I needed a job soon, because with my extravagant lifestyle (currently with many flights, Ayurveda, birthday and so on) I had little money in my account. So, Plan A was to find a job and stay there, Plan B was I didn't find one and had to travel back to Switzerland again. Plan B was never an option, not in my heart anyway, but it was a reasonable plan to fall back on. Fate would decide. This time I stayed in a small hotel that I had discovered during an earlier stay. The Bentota Inn is located, separated only by the railway line, on the beach of Bentota. I liked it because it was without frills and yet met my European standards of comfort and cleanliness. There were also treatment rooms and trained staff for Ayurveda treatments, which I did not use, but it was nice knowing I had the option. I was doing well, although I'd had a small operation in Switzerland and the wound was still fresh. I have always had many pigment spots all over my body and as I got older, they became more and more abundant. I was not sure if the Sri Lankan sun had caused any damage to my skin. Therefore, I had been to a dermatologist who looked at me from head to toe. He had no qualms about the spots that seemed suspicious to me. But he found an area below the left collarbone conspicuous and removed a bit for a biopsy. The result didn't sound good at all: there were a few cells there that could indicate skin cancer. Oh, dear, too much sun? To be honest, my sun protection had always been limited to avoiding direct sunlight. Which, logically, I couldn't consistently adhere to when I was riding my bike, for example. The dermatologist recommended that I remove the area in question, just to be on the safe side, which meant that I had to go under the knife again. There was a rather long scar, which was covered by a thick plaster, when I left for Sri Lanka.

Thus doctored, I came to the restaurant of the Bentota Inn on my first evening and stretched my swollen feet out in front of me. I was almost too tired to eat, but I wanted to get a taste of the wonderful evening air. Fried rice always went down a treat and I knew that I could sleep better with carbohydrates in my stomach. I grinned in the happiness of my return to paradise when I noticed a white woman at the next table, who was also alone. She was French and we quickly got into conversation – as with English, my French is rudimentary. Francine was in Sri Lanka because she was seeking healing. She had a difficult relationship with her husband in France and needed distance to decide how to proceed. In contrast to me, she used the Ayurveda offer of the hotel and had already recovered quite well in the last two weeks. She had even started to give treatments herself on a small scale: she was clairvoyant and had special abilities to give healing energy to people. Since she had started the journey with very little money, this gave her a small extra income and also rebuilt her battered self-confidence. We quickly became friends, because I too was very interested in healing and the supernatural. The next day we talked about my fresh wound and she offered to treat me - which of course I gladly accepted. In her room I stretched out on the bed and she listened to the information she received from the spiritual world. She treated me in silence and after an hour I was allowed to get up. I was quite exhausted, but so was she. 'What did you feel?' I now asked curiously. 'Oh,' she said, 'a lot of black magic!' I was shocked – black magic in me? I meditated regularly, was mostly optimistic, helpful (too much even, ahem) and a really decent person. No, she said, it wasn't my energy that was dark, it was some that was stuck in my energy field. Black magic that had been sent to me and which was also the reason for the precursors of skin cancer. Since the energy had landed in the area above my heart, she thought that there was a connection to the sender on that level. Someone with whom I had a heart relationship could have put a curse on me. I froze in fear. I could only think of one person who could be behind such a story: Chamara. Although he had completely sucked me dry financially and emotionally, he was deeply hurt that I did not support him any further. That I had dropped him. At that time, I still didn't know what he had done with my money, but I was now aware that he smoked cannabis heavily - several times a day and for about twenty years. I can't tell if cannabis is addictive. But I have the feeling that it feeds the dark sides that are slumbering in each of us. Like all intoxicants do. And that is as destructive as addiction. When you offer your shadow so much food, an inner monster grows out of it and takes over. In Chamara, the dark parts of him had already grown very large. It had a light core, but it was surrounded by thick, sweet smoke. Francine had had to work hard to energetically remove the curse that was attached to me. She strongly advised me to stay away from the guy, he was definitely not good for me. After a few days, I had a second session and she had much less work to do. I was on my way to health, on all levels. My wound healed well and to this day I do not see any signs of a new dark patch of skin, nor am I afraid of it. The subject is closed for me.

CHAPTER 26:

Plan A or Plan B

In addition to the healing work on myself, it was now, of course, important to find an income opportunity as soon as possible. I contacted a few people I knew from previous visits and was somehow directed to Bob. Bob was English and lived in Induruwa, south of Bentota. He was a retired teacher and long-time lover of Sri Lanka and had built up a small school. On the one hand, he had found a meaningful occupation for himself, and on the other hand, he was able to help children in Sri Lanka, which was important to him. In his small school he and an English colleague gave English lessons for people between four and sixteen years of age who wanted to learn. They had so many requests at that time that they were looking for help. What a happy coincidence! I immediately called Bob to apply for the job. English is not my mother tongue, but it would be enough for the little ones, I thought. The very next day we met and immediately liked each other. Bob asked if I would also teach German; they'd had to refuse requests from hotel employees who'd wished to learn German, as they didn't have a teacher. Sure, with pleasure, deal! Excited and full of joy, I returned to the Bentota Inn and celebrated my success with Francine. Fate had set a new course and I liked it a lot: it meant I could stay. Yay! Now I just had to find suitable accommodation. This could be difficult, I knew, because there were a few basic conditions that had to be fulfilled. The topic of security was important: as a woman living alone, I needed some kind of protection. I couldn't just rent a house like I do at home and trust that the boundaries of my property would be respected. I wanted to be able to sleep in peace. There were hardly any apartments in Sri Lanka, so I was looking for a house. A certain comfort was also important to me: I wanted my own bathroom, and for it to be inside the house (no shower in the garden, like many locals have). A washing machine would be great, especially for a longer stay. Quiet was also important; I didn't want to live directly on the main street. Since there were no houses directly at the beach, it had to be a house at the edge of the village, which was also within cycling distance from the school. In his time off, Bob drove me to some houses he knew were available. We didn't even get out of the car for half of them. The other half fell out of the race as soon as we stepped through the door: they weren't suitable at all! They were all old and dilapidated buildings which I did not want to move into under any circumstances. When we were both tired and wanted to give up, the solution came: the best in the end! Friends of Bob, an English couple, were waiting for us. It was a house with a special story, and that story would play an important role. But more about that later! Here is what we saw: the whole property was surrounded by an intact, freshly painted wall, the house was not visible from the outside. A heavy metal sliding gate opened after our ringing and Bob drove his car onto the gravel road of the driveway. We got out of the car and were welcomed by the owners. After some small talk and the typical English wisecracks, they showed us around the property. I saw a big two-storey villa with huge windows and sliding doors opening onto the garden. Everything was very spacious and beautifully arranged. From the veranda, we had a great view into the garden, full of flowers and bushes. The lawn was very well maintained and pleasant under my bare feet. But the coolest thing was the mega giant swimming pool that immediately attracted me with its glittering blue. A pool, a pool, a pool! This was where I wanted to live, it was clear right away! But which part of the house was for rent? Only at the end of the tour we came to a small outbuilding that was attached to the main house and at first sight looked like a garage. A small house with two rooms, kitchen and bathroom, which was actually built for employees and completely furnished. It was therefore also called Staff Bungalow. The English offered it to me to rent. Could you believe it? The price was in line with the salary I would earn at school: I would have to invest about a third of my 400 euros. But hello, there was really no question of having to. It was a dream! And it was topped by the fact that there were two dogs to keep me company. They were the only survivors of a whole litter; their siblings had sadly been eaten by a monitor lizard. The English couple themselves had dogs at home and their love of animals left them no choice: they took the two orphaned babies to their holiday home. A local family, who also took care of the garden and pool, had looked after the pups, and they had become big beautiful ladies. I was more than happy and thought not only of the company but also of the security that the presence of the dogs would give me. I still thank you today, Luna and Ginger, for your company, protection, and comfort. Also, thanks to your unconditional love my heart could heal again. Plan A was fulfilled and only ten days after my arrival I saw what title the next chapter of my life would have: My life as a teacher in Sri Lanka, and as a woman of luxury in a villa with a pool. Life was beautiful again!

CHAPTER 27:

My Life as a Teacher in Sri Lanka

I was pretty excited when I started my new job. Luckily, there were books at school that I could use as a teacher, so I didn't have to make up the lesson material on my own. But the children didn't have any books. For many parents, raising money for the lessons was the maximum they could offer their children. Books were a luxury. So, we copied, made collages, played games - creativity was needed to keep the children happy. They all had English on their timetable, every day. And they all still couldn't make a complete sentence in that language. I couldn't believe it at first and thought about spending an hour as a guest in the public school. I wanted to understand how their lessons went and why they learned absolutely nothing there. But after passing by a classroom and hearing what was going on inside, I had no need and no illusions: it was pure chaos! I could see it through the open door: the furniture was made of the simplest raw wooden planks, and the tables were so narrow that an A4 sheet of paper could only fit across them. I wouldn't have lasted ten minutes on the benches, they looked so uncomfortable. The teacher droned on at them, a pure monologue. The students talked, threw paper, played, made mischief. How terrible it must have been for a child to spend many hours a day in an atmosphere that killed all interest and enthusiasm. They couldn't take in anything anymore; they had to close down at some point, even if they were eager to learn. But I think it went even further: the children developed such an aversion to the English language that they could hardly be motivated to learn. They had resigned themselves and dragged themselves reluctantly through the extra lessons in the afternoon. But without knowledge of English, the chances of getting a job are even lower than they were anyway, especially in an area like Bentota, which lives on tourism. The tutoring should give the children a better chance to earn money and support their families! To my horror I also had to realise that they did not learn how to learn at all. They did not develop any initiative of their own, expected to be fed and carried somehow and then suddenly to be able to talk in English. Fortunately, there were a few good examples of willing pupils, but the majority of the students were lethargic. Discipline was difficult, even for the adults; the children showed up regularly, but the adults did not. There were a thousand and one excuses, and they seldom signed off when they couldn't come. I only found out the following week what the reason for their absence was. Here is a small selection of the excuses: it had rained, someone in the village had died, someone in the neighbouring village had died, they had to go to a wedding (which always took place during the day), the mother was ill, the grandmother was ill, they themselves were ill, and so on. There were still a lot of important things that stood in the way of participation. Since there were only a few participants in my German classes, sometimes nobody showed up at all because of the emergencies, and I sat alone in the class. That was extremely annoying, because I didn't know whether they would come late or not at all. If I had come especially for the class, I was annoyed. Yes, I, as a teacher, could come to school even when it was raining, even if I only had a bicycle. This excuse did not apply to me. I often found it terribly unsatisfying! But there were also many moments that were really fun and in which I realised that I could give something to my students. Then everyone was happy.

Very difficult, for both sides, were of course mistakes that had already been firmly anchored in their memories over the years and were therefore difficult to unlearn. Sri Lankan teachers rarely speak grammatically correct English: for example, it was a great test of patience for me to establish articles. In their everyday life, my students mostly spoke Sinhala, the official language of the country. Sinhalese make up the majority of the population (75 percent), while Tamils (and foreigners) make up the rest. Tamil is a separate language with different characters than Sinhala. Words are often seen written in three languages, for example on buses and place-name signs: Sinhala, Tamil and English. Quite a lot of work! I taught the children in English and the adults in German. I took lessons myself in order to learn Sinhala and so I was able to understand many difficulties of my students better. In their language, for example, there are no articles in front of the nouns, so instead of 'Please give me an apple,' they just say, 'Give me apple'. The fact that 'a' before a vowel becomes 'an' was apparently completely new to them, and they had difficulties with it. And please is also not used so often in

Sinhala. The word for please is also a bit long: karunakara. This is spoken with emphasis on the third syllable and then sounds like a sung invitation to do something. But then, mostly it falls under the table and the sentence is reduced to the essence of: 'Give me apple!' I explained to them that this is different with Europeans and that we (especially in Switzerland) attach great importance to politeness and a please is part of it. Another problem was the choice of topics I was able to work on with the children: we worked with books that had been produced in the West. They showed everyday scenes of families in England, Australia, or other countries with a different standard of living. There were chapters that dealt with eating habits and cooking. A child in Sri Lanka never helps in the kitchen (as far as I have experienced); no matter if they are a girl or boy, the children never help with cooking. The girls learn it quite late, and I did not meet anybody at school who had an idea of how to prepare food. So how should I bring this up? In our books, games were suggested in which people cooked. Recipes were printed and we were supposed to make whole sentences and write a little story out of them. A fitted kitchen was illustrated, and the children should know the words of the cupboards and appliances in English. I don't think that there were kitchen cupboards in many Sri Lankan households at all. Cooking was done everywhere on gas stoves, sometimes even on a wood fire; there were no ovens, and the dining table served as a work surface. In the end, I left that chapter out completely. Instead, I continued to develop other chapters, to which everyone could relate. For example, the topic of food. Coincidentally, also my favourite subject. In our conversations, I learned a lot about the eating habits of the Sri Lankans. I was very fond of asking my students, 'What do you eat at home?' and the classroom began to come to life. For breakfast, there were a great many different things: rice pudding (cooked in coconut milk) with a side dish of raw chopped onions, chili, salt and lime juice. Or also with sugar. Or they ate string hoppers, a kind of spaghetti made of rice flour, water, salt and oil. The mass was used to make small flat thread nests with a press, which were then put into a steamer. The production is quite complex and often these hoppers are not homemade but bought at small stalls at the roadside or in bakeries. You could eat hot coconut sambal (with chili) or a mild curry with curry leaves with it. Egg-hoppers are also popular: a wafer-thin, crispy pancake made from rice flour and coconut milk and covered with a fried egg. And again: a hot sambal for dipping or rolling up. Some families, on the other hand, preferred pieces of fresh white bread in the morning, which they dipped into a fish, potato, or egg curry. My mouth is watering while writing this – I liked the Sri Lankan breakfasts very much, actually in all variations. Unfortunately, in the hotels, one often only gets the international tourist breakfast with fruit plate, toast, portioned jam, omelette and sliced cheese, which I think is a pity. In my bungalow, I liked to make a curry of yellow lentils in the mornings; this was very fast. I also ate fluffy white bread, which I could buy fresh every day on every corner, and a fried egg. I also had Ceylon tea and fresh papaya juice, which was healthy and tasty and gave me energy until noon. The children then ate rice and curry for lunch, and rice and curry again in the evening, or even Kottu. This dish is available at many street stalls and you can recognise the Kottu cooks from far away by the noise they make. It sounds like a quick hammering tacktacktack. It is made when Roti (coconut pancakes) are chopped, mixed and fried together with vegetables and spices on a hot metal plate.

Delicious! When I asked the children what their favourite food was, 80 percent said rice and curry and 20 percent said Kentucky Fried Chicken or McDonald's, which they knew from one of their rare visits to Colombo. That was all they knew; they were not spoiled in this regard.

It was just as difficult with lessons about hobbies as with conversations about excursions. The children rarely had a hobby. But since they were asked again and again in school: 'What is your favourite subject?' some resourceful ones started to say, 'I am collecting stamps,' or, 'I enjoy painting,' both of which I strongly doubted. The boys all without exception liked to play cricket, some football, and that was it. And they watched soaps. Whole families would sit in front of the screen every day to see their heroes crying and laughing. There were many local soaps, but also surprisingly many Japanese series with actors in stiff traditional dresses, with serious expressions on their faces. The Sri Lankans loved them. The women actually only left their homes to visit other families or to go shopping, and that was together with their husbands. By the way, they (by this I mean all of them: husband and wife and children) rarely went to the beach, never swam, rarely went to the cinema or to exhibitions, and they did not play any sports (except cricket and football). I would very rarely see a lonely cyclist who, in the relative coolness of the morning, did his miles on the coastal road. Or even groups of men who met in the evening for a walk on the beach or for volleyball. While parents in Western countries take their offspring to all sorts of different activities, which are intended to develop their skills and also be fun, Sri Lankan parents take their children to tutoring sessions - up to five times a week. This leaves little time for anything else. The mothers often waited near the school or in the reception area because they did not want to leave their children alone. Mother and child were then picked up together by a tuktuk, which was driven either by a family member or a good friend. I have never seen women behind the wheel of a tuktuk. Cars were only owned by a few guides or hotel owners. In Sri Lanka, whole families travel either in a tuktuk, on a motorbike or the good old bicycle. Yes, one good old bicycle! I was amazed how many people could fit on it. On the first day after the school holidays, there were few children who had ever made even a small trip and left the village or travelled elsewhere in their country. A trip to the tooth temple in Kandy, to the highest Buddhist sanctuary was always a duty and something very special. As mentioned before, this temple is said to hold a tooth of Buddha and the Buddhists worship this place. Every year in August, this highest relic is carried through the place in a procession with decorated elephants as part of a ten-day festival. A trip to Kandy is usually made with the whole family or with friends. For this purpose, a minibus is rented, because there is a lot of luggage and provisions to transport. I even once saw a group that was on the way in a public bus. Probably a family member worked as a bus driver and could use the bus for two or three days. Everything is possible and necessity is the mother of invention! Since it is too far to go to the highlands for a day trip, the families stay in hotels on the way, where many people share a room and beds. This is a party in Sri Lanka!

In the highlands, you get into completely different climates; here, it is always green and there is a lot of fog and cold. Kandy (the former royal city) is situated at an altitude of 500 metres, the city of Nuwara Eliya even higher at 1800 metres. Here, you are in the middle of the tea plantations where the famous

Ceylon Tea is harvested. The people who live here must be tough, because the climate is as tough as their work. When Sri Lankans talk about this area, they always start trembling – it is really extremely cold for them. It cools down to eighteen degrees during the day, at night even to seven. Compared to the beach climate, this feels like the North Pole, and fleece shirts and down jackets are offered everywhere and are gladly bought. If a student had been on such an excursion, there was of course a lot to tell after the school holidays. Very rarely a student could tell about a stay abroad; that was a sensation. Sri Lanka is fairly isolated, with only India and the Maldives nearby. And why bother flying to the Maldives? There are enough beaches and sea in Sri Lanka. I often felt sorry for my students when I saw how restricted their life was. Fortunately, they knew nothing else and suffered much less than I imagined. The challenge for me was to find a subject in which they could use their English vocabulary. But I always found something, and we really had a lot of fun. Animals were popular, plants, fruit and vegetables, colours and numbers. And then there were lots of verbs and many secrets of grammar. I never really liked prepositions in my own English lessons and my students were no different: above, across, of, on, towards, to, and similar harassment. Not easy. So, there was a lot to practice. All in all, I was happy with my job, I was among people, had a daily schedule, occasionally felt successful, could be creative, and earned money. Having work that was not difficult allowed me to spend my energy on my inner work. I had time to digest, integrate, and overcome my experiences. Step by step.

Our school did not yet have any textbooks for the German lessons. Therefore, I contacted the Goethe Institute in Colombo and found out which ones were used there. Most of the German students were adults and worked in one of the many hotels in and around Bentota. Some were also married to German women and wanted to emigrate to Germany. Before leaving the country, they had to apply for a visa, and to do so, they had to pass a German test. And they could take it at the Goethe Institute. So, it made sense that I got the same books and worked towards my students (or at least the better students) being able to take their exams in Colombo. I liked the German books very much, because they described situations from our everyday life in Germany or Switzerland. For the Sri Lankans, this was also an introduction to a foreign culture. I often gave them practical examples where the difference between the two countries struck me particularly. Shopping in Switzerland would go like this: the shop assistant says: '40.50 francs, please.' I give her 42 francs and she says, 'Thank you,' then she gives me 1.50 francs change and I thank her again. 'Have a nice day!' (Or afternoon or evening.) The Swiss are always very polite; in Germany the procedure can be a bit more casual. In Sri Lanka, however, it is all very time-saving, short and to the point, with two words: '250 rupees!' No thank you, no request, nothing. I always found it very unfriendly, even after months. Just like the jostling everywhere: the join the queue of the British has never set foot on Sri Lankan soil. In the bank, there was a line on the floor indicating where the next customer should wait. We also know it in our own country; it's all about the protection of privacy. But why do you need privacy, who has secrets here? There are usually as many people standing close together at the counter as there is room for. You hear everything, see everything, know everything. When a Sri Lankan leaves the bank building, he doesn't hold the door open for the next person. It doesn't matter if someone walks right behind him: the door swings open and closes again and slams the next person right in his face. Then suddenly there was no more togetherness, there was only me. There was so much that was strange to me and I humorously explained the differences to my students, because I wanted them to understand that there are different customs in other countries. And yes, I thought they might be able to change theirs a little, admittedly. After all, in the end, who would ever be able to travel to Europe and experience it for themselves? The visa conditions are extremely difficult and many sadly fail the German test. The authorities have probably already seen too many people who left the country not to come back. Many Sri Lankans hope and pray all their lives in vain and will never leave their island. This realisation made me very grateful for the fact that I was allowed to experience so much freedom and to get to know other countries and customs.

CHAPTER 28:

The Villa

Besides settling in at the school, I began to settle in my new home. I still couldn't believe that I had so much luck. Rick and Maureen, who owned the villa, travelled back to England after we spent a few days together; their holiday was over. They locked the main house but kindly left the laundry room door open for me to use. Now I had my little villa and the lush garden all to myself. The dogs were very sweet and probably as happy to have company as I was. They were not used to walking on a leash and so they always stayed inside the walls where they had enough exercise. Well, mostly always ... Actually, I wasn't supposed to let them out, but they were fast like greyhounds and did everything they could to slip through the gate with me when it was open. I had a soft heart and could understand their urge for movement and variety, so I let them out from time to time. They would roam around and only come back when they were hungry. Since there was only a narrow concrete path leading to our house, on which the neighbours rode a bicycle or tuktuk every now and then, I trusted that nothing would happen to the dogs, and I was lucky.

I took good care of the dogs when we were together. Once a day, I cooked rice with chicken necks, and sometimes I fetched a beef heart from the market (this was rather rare, I didn't get along with the smell and the flies there). They were wonderful companions and I finally felt not so alone anymore. The best thing about the time in the villa was of course the pool! Every day I swam my laps and I loved it when one of the dogs lay at the edge of the pool and waited for me. The sun in Sri Lanka was so hot that the water could even be unpleasantly warm - and I had to be careful not to get a sunburn. Because although I normally avoided the sun, this did not work in the pool, because it was not covered. My favourite times to swim were in the early morning or even at night. I have an especially intense memory of one night in particular: it was a full moon in a starry sky, warm, and I was alone in the pool, protected from curious looks. I lay stark naked in the warm water, spreading my arms and legs like a starfish so that I floated motionless on the surface of the water. I was one with everything: with heaven and earth, with the animals, the water and the air. There was no time and no space, there was no I and no you. There was only oneness and it was beautiful! I will never forget this moment; it rests in me like a precious treasure.

But the walls that surrounded me offered only apparent security. This wasn't just about burglars. There were other types of intruders, and unfortunately, the walls were useless against them. Another person had access to my paradise, and he was not friendly to me. I now must explain something about the history of this place: Rick and Maureen had stayed seven years earlier as tourists in a hotel on Bentota Beach. They loved the country and could well imagine having their own house there. As it was to happen, one fine day they met Rasta, who was waiting for customers on the beach. He had his own tuktuk and offered himself for excursions and everything a tourist heart could desire. The three of them became friends and soon the subject came up to buy a plot of land. Of course, Rasta had some ideas, he knew some people and drove Rick and Maureen around to see them. They fell in love with a plot of land on the edge of the village and bought it. It was the land where I was living now. I don't know who exactly was registered in the land registry (which is an issue because of the tax). Only the English buyers paid, of course. It was their land and they built their house. They designed their dream villa and accomplished the first steps in building it, then they had to go back to their work in England. Rasta was now the man on the spot. He enjoyed their full confidence and over time became like a son to them. The villa was finished, the English came for their first holiday in their new vacation home, and everyone was happy. Rasta moved into the staff bungalow and now had a regular income, taking care of the pool, garden and dogs. A princely situation for a man who had lived in very simple circumstances until then. And it got even better: Rasta met a woman from Germany on the beach and the two fell in love. After a few months and repeated visits to the woman in Bentota, they got married. It couldn't have been any better! The long procedure with language course and visa application needed patience, but went without any problems and Rasta was ready for a new life in Germany. Now the question was who would take over his job and who would live in his bungalow. But, actually it was not really a question for Rasta, because there were unwritten rules for such cases. In Sri Lanka, that is, not in England. Rasta, as the eldest son of his biological family, appointed his younger brother, Rajith, as his successor. Rajith expected nothing else and had already become well-acquainted with the idea. The English, however, had not thought of such an arrangement at all! They were looking for a solution when Bob told them I was looking for a flat. And they thought it was brilliant timing that I would show up and take this place. Now this was a tricky situation. From the Sri Lankan point of view, Rasta, and therefore, Rajith belonged with the English family and not just virtually, but completely. They were part of the family, not me! I came from outside and wanted to take away the source of so much good from them. Of course, they were not enthusiastic. But Rick and Maureen made a decision: I was allowed to move into the bungalow. They offered Rajith the job of cleaning the pool and taking care of the garden for a monthly salary. Sounds good, right? But it sounded like an insult to the Sri Lankans. Rajith was no employee, he was family! If his brother was like a son to the English, he was like a son to them, he thought. And, very badly, the brothers lost face in front of their friends, for this was a clear descent on the social ladder. And this was difficult, this was unacceptable. Of course, I didn't know about these confusions at the beginning; I think even the English could not foresee the consequences of their decision. I was just amazed that Rajith was so hostile towards me from day one. It took several months and an introduction to Sri Lankan culture by European friends to understand this. When Rasta heard about these arrangements in faraway Germany, he insulted his adoptive parents on the phone and forbade his brother to take the job. Either he was allowed to live in the bungalow and do the job, or nothing at all. It was a tough back and forth across the globe and ended with Rajith agreeing to do the job after all, even without the right of residence.

So, I started my stay in the beautiful house in a very tense atmosphere. My relationship with Rajith only relaxed when I moved out again. But many months passed until then and I often managed to hide when he was around. I was constantly put to the test, because he appeared unannounced whenever it suited him. He had the keys to the gate and the main house, and my stomach contracted every time I heard a tuktuk drive up. He was always in a grim mood. Actually, he spoke good German, but he insisted that I speak English with him. I think he felt more confident in his English abilities. He demonstrated his affiliation with the villa and at the same time his independence in different ways: as I said, he came and went when he wanted. He liked to come in the evening, and I was not eager to be alone with him on the property when it got dark. He often had red eyes, liked to drink and was quick-tempered - and emotionally hurt. I was afraid of him, but had to live with his presence and sometimes longed for it, because the pool had to be cleaned regularly in the heat. The chemicals had to be refilled, otherwise algae would form. I had green water several times and couldn't use the pool, but didn't know how to clean it, so I had to wait until it suited him to come back. Sometimes I called him and asked when that would be. Then he was supposed to be on a tour with guests and couldn't come for a few days. This could be true and he was really on the other side of the island, or he was right next door, only he knew the truth. A totally stupid game and I was dependent on him. I was ready to learn how to clean the pool, but I didn't want to take away his job either, because that would have only increased the tension. But the most important thing for me was that I was safe from him and his moods. Should I go into the confrontation or give in? The English saw themselves powerless in this situation and were far away. There was no real support from them. Also annoying were the evenings when he did with his buddies what he had probably wanted to do regularly before I showed up: throw a pool party. It could happen that in the evening the gate suddenly opened and some tuktuks containing him and some friends drove in. They were loafing around the pool, drinking Arrak and smoking ganja, listening to music. Since Rajith had the key to the main villa, they could go to the big kitchen and cook their dinner there. When everyone was happy, they would go into the pool and it would get cheerfully loud. I wanted them to have fun with all my heart, really. But I asked Rajith to let me know beforehand if he was planning such parties. My request was rejected. He said I wasn't his boss. And he was right. At the same time, I understood that in Sri Lanka everything is spontaneous. It could well be that it was only in the afternoon that they had the idea to meet at the villa. Okay, but even then, there was still time to call me. He just didn't want to; it was his house and he didn't owe me an explanation.

One morning I had cooked the food for the dogs on my stove and forgot to turn off the gas. The pot was still on the fire when, luckily, Rajith showed up to do the garden. He noticed smoke coming out of my kitchen and was able to prevent worse things than the pot being ruined. After that he called me immediately at school and barked into the telephone 'Did you want to burn the house down?!' Every word was thrown at me like an arrow. It was only the third time he repeated himself that I understood what he meant, and I sank into the ground with guilt. It was absolutely my fault; it shouldn't have happened! This suited him well again. It was a shitty game we were playing, and I didn't know what to do. I tried to talk to Rajith, try to explain to him that I didn't want to get in his way. That he still had his place in the villa, but now I needed one too. He stared at me with a closed face and I realised once again what I so often experienced with Sri Lankans: they were not used to solving conflicts verbally. They were more used to fighting. They have a great pride that can be hurt very easily. Plus: they can be resentful. What can you do about it? Not much, except be patient until he can change. For a woman from Northern Germany who likes to find a solution directly and quickly, there was a lot to learn. And I learned a lot in that time, I had no choice. But it had to escalate first, to finally become more relaxed between Rajith and me. Like a pressure cooker, which has to release pressure in order not to explode, our situation also needed a valve.

And this happened unexpectedly, as it so often does. One evening, Rajith was on the property and I had approached him for something, I forget what. Did I need help with something in my bungalow? Yes, I think the gas bottle was empty and I didn't know how to get a new one and how to connect it. I didn't know anything about gas stoves. That's probably why he was in the kitchen with me. Anyway, our conversation somehow escalated into a duel of words. He was just leaving when he turned around once more and put his foot in the door so that I couldn't close it. His eyes turned red and he shouted 'I will throw you over the wall!' as he fixed me with a look filled with hatred. Okay, he didn't actually throw me over the wall, and I somehow managed to stay calm. After a short time, I was able to end the conversation and close the door, trembling with fear. Of course, I knew that in Sri Lanka threats are the order of the day and rarely anything really happens. And I also knew that his hurt ego only wanted to demonstrate power to me. But it was a fact that the guy was stoned or drunk and his feelings were only controlled by a thin layer of rationale (or whatever). And, not to forget, he had the key to the gate and could come back at any time, even with reinforcements. I had to get out of there! I quickly packed a few things and, completely terrified, I grabbed my bike and left the property. It was already dark. Where could I go? No friends for miles around to go to. My teacher colleagues lived too far away for a night out. I wanted to go to a hotel with lights on and familiar faces. Where I could tell my story and where I would be safe. I planned to stay there for a few days and let the situation cool down. Then I would see clearly. I made my way to the Bentota Inn where I had spent my first two weeks of this stay. The German manager was still up, and I immediately burst into tears when I saw him. After two glasses of Arrak all my misery broke out of me and I told him about the constant tension I was under and my fear. He too was of the opinion that surely nothing would happen, but who knows? I was infinitely relieved that I was safe and could fall asleep at some point. The next day I had to work, fortunately it was not far to school. There my colleagues listened to my story and I calmed down more and more. They, too, had already experienced threats, and nothing had happened. It was a strange country where we all lived voluntarily. And again, the question arose: what kept us there so stubbornly, when it was so difficult? It was good to exchange ideas. Then I wrote a text message to my landlords and asked them to clarify the situation. They phoned Rajith, but there was nothing they could do. It was something between him and me. I stayed in the hotel for three nights, only dropping by briefly during the day to feed the dogs. Then I felt stable enough to return to my apartment. I was not relaxed, but somehow it went better afterwards. My landlords paid me back for the hotel expenses when they came to visit the next time, but that was not really the most important part of the lesson. I had to learn to be strong, to stand my ground. A quality that was still a shadowy existence in me. But I grew, I firmly resolved to see this as a school of life and to accept my experiences as my teachers. And so it went. Fortunately, I was never threatened again.

CHAPTER 29:

Let Go

Of course, the story with the Dolphin Villa and Chamara was not yet finished in my heart. Only very slowly I realised what had happened to me. And, of course, our separation didn't go as smoothly as it seemed until now. A former beach boy doesn't give up that easily! He was tough and he pulled out all the stops of flattery. Like a player, he intuitively grasped the situation, sensed where my weaknesses were and acted tactically smart. Just as I had experienced him at the gaming table with the ladies from Israel, he went through his life - and partly through mine. When I was still in Switzerland, he had called and messaged a few times: 'Honey, we have a high electricity bill. Could you please send 400 francs with Western Union?!' I must admit, I did it once. I couldn't believe that my money was really gone, that I had been fooled so much. I thought, okay, now grit your teeth again and keep fighting, at some point the tide will turn and money will come back. Eventually the hotel will run. Our hotel. I remember when I stayed at my mother's house at Christmas and on Christmas Eve, I sorted the booking requests for my hotel, because it was really starting to work. My efforts had improved the internet presence of the Dolphin Villa and the hotel got good reviews. We had some bookings and I was euphoric that everything seemed to be improving. However, Chamara and I did not have regular contact and I tried very hard to distance myself from him in my heart as well. I had finally handed over the administration of the bookings to him in February, despite my fear that he would not take care of it. It was all so unclear, so unresolved, but I had my signature on our contract. I could hold on to that. Ten months later, when I was living in Sri Lanka again, I had a driver who I knew from previous visits pick me up from the airport. We chatted the long way to my hotel and exchanged news about mutual acquaintances. Quite casually he said at some point: 'Chamara has sold the hotel, the owner of the Blue Lagoon Hotel has taken it. That's what he always wanted. Yeah, too bad Chamara didn't make it.' I was completely taken by surprise and I felt really, really sick. I couldn't believe it! I didn't know a thing. I never heard a word about it. He had lied to me in many ways, but this was the real deal! And of course, the fear came up immediately: will I ever get my money back? How was he going to make enough money to pay me back my loan without the hotel? During the time I was looking for a job and accommodation, I had to clarify this issue further. I went to Colombo and met with a lawyer experienced in fraud cases with foreigners. Until then, I knew only a few similar fates, but this man had seen a lot of them. I had brought the contract that Chamara had signed and presented it to the lawyer. He said, yes, it was a valid document. But, he said, 'Madam, forget your money, let it go!' He had seen this kind of situation too many times before. His experience was that the cheated foreign woman had no chance of ever seeing her money again. The lawyers involved would delay the proceedings until the woman was financially and emotionally at an end, because that way they too could still get a piece of the pie. Each trial filled their coffers and emptied those of the cheated woman even more. And the probability that Chamara would really be able to pay his debts in ten years - especially in the amount of several millions - was ZERO. 'Decide for your health, Madam, let go!' He said this emphatically. It was hard to hear, but I felt he was right. I had already suffered a lot, but now I had to wake up and pull myself out of the pain. It hurt. I had been so incredibly stupid, blind with love and gullible. And the worst thing: I could apparently not trust my inner voice! She had said loud and clear: it's okay! Trust him, he is the man of your dreams, everything is fine! How should I trust my intuition in future decisions? What to build my life on, if not on my inner guidance? That was intense.

I knew I was badly hurt, and I wanted to heal. I wanted to be free from the overwhelming emotions and finally be happy. I did not want to perish from an incurable cancer because my hatred was eating me up inside. So, I decided to use the time in the villa with the pool for my healing. Slowly to say goodbye in my heart to my illusion of having a hotel in Sri Lanka. Farewell to the joy of having a life partner, farewell to the red-hot anger at Chamara. And goodbye to the equally intense vicious rage against myself. I avoided further meetings and did not answer his messages anymore. Finally, I was able to draw a line. I cried a lot, I was sad, I found distance - slowly but steadily. Today I am writing these lines free of anger. After a few years there is only a very distant dull pain, and it becomes less and less. Writing does me good.

When I was living in the villa with the dogs, I was still chewing on some things that were not clear to me about my ex. I got up the courage to meet the new owner of the Blue Lagoon. He knew me. My connection with the Dolphin Villa was well known - nothing is kept secret in Sri Lanka. I met him on the beach outside his hotel and we sat together. He told me that he had indeed been waiting for a long time for the opportunity to buy the Dolphin Villa. But Chamara had always refused. They were friends from school and had always wanted to outdo each other. He had hoped we would make it together, Chamara and I, but he knew him much better. There was another woman who had lived at the Dolphin Villa before I did and had been involved with Chamara. A Russian woman, he confirmed. She had also invested a lot of money and received nothing in return. He told me that she threatened to kill him to this day. It seemed she hadn't let go yet. And he finally gave me the piece of the puzzle that explained everything. The one I'd been looking for and which could clear up the fog in my head: Chamara was a gambling addict. He had only invested a small part of my money in the hotel. He had gambled it away! He put money into horse and dog racing. And he played cards every night - and lost, of course. Lots of money, every rupee he could get his hands on. His wife and daughter lived in a ruin without windows and running water, and he brought everything to the betting offices in Galle and Aluthgama. I was so shocked; I really couldn't find the words to say. I knew immediately that this man was telling the truth, because my subconscious put the whole picture together in seconds and everything suddenly made sense: my observations in the evenings when we had played cards together. His disappearance every evening: he hadn't gone to his wife's or to his parents' house, he had been gambling. Kumara, who had a private audience with him every morning and had been my bodyguard for some days, had been his close confidant and helper. He got daily my money and Chamara's bets into his hands and went off to bet the money. On dogs and horses. Maybe the boss himself was banned from gambling in the shops, I don't know. And I owed his company to the boss's order to seal me off from everyone who knew about it. It was just as well that he hardly spoke any English, so I couldn't interrogate him. Everything made sense now! I asked for a glass of Arrak and a cigarette and sat dumbfounded. It was a deep shock! I was grateful to the new owner of the Dolphin Villa for his honesty. At last I could stop brooding. After a while I had to get up, I just wanted to leave. I got on my bike and rode home as fast as I could. Just crying. Shit, my money was really gone! I had to let go of a lot more than just my ex-boyfriend.

CHAPTER 30:

Love Heals

I then caught myself again (and again and again...) and began the difficult work of forgiveness. This process was repeatedly interrupted by the emergence of a huge rage. Man, was I pissed off! I was fucking angry, I was deeply hurt, I was broken. My heart must have had a scar. I was banging on cushions, writing letters of abuse that I burned, and screaming my rage into the wind on the beach. And so it slowly diminished. And I began the long process of forgiving him and myself. A little more every day. I didn't want to waste any more of my energy. It was a very good decision, the right one for me! I can recommend this kind of healing to everyone. It takes some overcoming to forgive. Because it means giving up your role as a victim. It doesn't mean you approve of each other's actions. Chamara made a big mistake. But I wanted to forgive him so I could be free. Because anger is an umbilical cord that connects people. It meant a lot of work, I had to constantly observe my thoughts and feelings and direct them into the right direction. When anger appeared or when self-pity came up, I turned the wheel again and again in the direction of forgiveness. It hurt for a long time, for years, but it was a tactic that helped me to heal. I wanted to be able to look myself in the eyes again and love myself, and, very slowly, I succeeded.

In the middle of this process I started a new relationship with a man. Yes, a local man. This also helped him to get well, because love heals all wounds. I had really not intended to get involved with a Sri Lankan man again. But it did me good - even if it was not without turbulences, of course! I was allowed to experience a few romantic moments in the country of my dreams after all. He worked at the Kingfisher Hotel and Restaurant as a driver. His pride and joy was a black tuktuk, which he had leased and for which he had to pay almost all his wages. He had decorated it very nicely so that he could use it for tourist weddings. It was then decorated with balloons and took the bridal couple to the beach and back to the hotel. A wedding carriage, Sri Lanka style. The thing made quite the impression, with its leather seats and the big stereo. Bandula loved music. He proudly sat at the wheel of his stylish vehicle when he drove hotel guests to Aluthgama to the market or to other places of interest. He had a job he liked. However, he had to be available from eight o'clock in the morning until late at night - until finally all guests of the restaurant were safely back in their rooms. Unimaginable to Westerners, this sort of schedule, but it was everyday life in Sri Lanka. He was entitled to one day off per week, but this could also be cancelled or postponed at short notice if guests wanted to go on an excursion and he was needed. I had been to the Kingfisher Restaurant a few times and he had driven me home afterwards. With the bicycle, it was too dangerous for me in the dark on the shore road. He spoke English, but not very well. It was enough for the bare essentials, which was fine on our tuktuk trips. After he drove me a few times, he summoned all his courage one evening and asked if he could come and visit me. He would bring a bottle of Arrak and we could have a cosy evening at the pool. Hmm, I thought, why not? Since I liked having visitors and I liked him, I agreed. We arranged to meet for one day the following week, and I was looking forward to the evening. I cooked something for us and dressed nicely, organised music, and then it was time. Bandula had obviously also dressed up and wore a nice ironed Hawaiian shirt instead of the usual t-shirt, of course with Bermuda shorts and flipflops. He parked his tuktuk inside the walls of my villa and I had to lock up my animal roommates because, like so many Sri Lankans, he was afraid of dogs. No problem. We made ourselves comfortable, drank and talked...for a little while. Because we ran out of things to talk about pretty soon. 'Very nice place,' ... 'English people very nice,' ... 'You .... are very beautiful,' ..... 'I ....love Bob Marley,'.......... The pauses got longer and longer, so we drank a little more. I had dealt with this moment in advance, so it didn't come out of nowhere when I confidently announced: 'I want to have sex with you; would you like it?' I had the feeling that it didn't really come as a surprise to him either, because he didn't hesitate for a second.

I know it sounds very strange considering what I had experienced so far and the traps I had fallen into before. I had no intention of being hurt again. I wanted to finally enjoy myself! I saw other women being free and taking lovers. I had decided that I wanted to enjoy this pleasure too. I was now fifty years old and had no partner, I liked sex and here was a man who liked it - and me too. So why not?! We went into my bedroom and quickly found each other. When we sank down on my bed, Bandula sighed, 'Now you are mine,' which I didn't want to comment on at that moment, but I had to clarify later. After sex and a shower, we continued our silence at the pool and drank a little more. Later we made love again under the starry sky. I was happy, it was almost too beautiful after all the drama with Chamara. Bandula was a sweet teddy bear with beautiful dark skin, lots of hair - and a round, cuddly body. He loved to be touched and to caress me with his soft hands. We explored and enjoyed each other there on the pool deck. An evening full of pleasure! When I later opened the gate for him, we found freshly torn-off branches that clearly indicated that someone had climbed over the wall. Someone had been watching us! So much for the protection by the walls. I hadn't thought of that possibility at all. Well, it couldn't be helped, but I had a queasy feeling, because I didn't want the audience to think that I was easy prey. That Bandula would spend the night with me was never in question. Because we agreed that not everybody had to know that we 'had something together'. Besides, he was just a lover to me, nothing more. That's what I had agreed with myself. But, of course, I had decided on this casual status without consulting him. Now you are mine ...

From then on, I was inundated with declarations of love. He seldom called me, because his job left him very little free time. But every day he sent a loving text message. It took a few weeks until I found out that the texts were not from him. His best friend wrote the words and sent them first to Bandula, who then forwarded them to me. I always made it clear to him that I didn't love him, which was true, and that I only wanted sex. 'Okay darling okay, no problem, I like sex with you.' But it was clear that there was a lot more emotion involved for him than for me. And, of course, expectations. Having a relationship with a European woman brought many possibilities within reach for him in his mind: travel, money, support, regular sex, maybe even marriage. It did not make a difference that he knew my story and should have known my financial situation: somehow, he still thought that I was rich. There seems to be the idea that money grows on trees in Europe. White equals rich. In truth, I could afford things in Sri Lanka that Bandula could never buy. His meagre salary was already spent on the tuktuk. If he was lucky, he was tipped by the customers he drove around. In the off-season he had no trips for weeks, so he had no extra income. Then he helped out in the hotel when there was need and went shopping for the restaurant. Bandula lived in the house of his brother, who was married and had two daughters. Once, he showed me his bed, a cot in a kind of storage room next to the kitchen. The whole house had no plaster on the walls; his corner was dark and looked terribly uncomfortable. But - maybe that wasn't his bed at all. Although this living situation was presented to me as a fact, in the course of time I kept hearing comments from colleagues who said: 'No, he lives in his old parents' house, at the end of the street.' Or 'He lives with a friend.' Bandula's truth was this: the house actually belonged - supposedly - to him; he had inherited it, but then left it to his brother, because he had family. And Bandula was single ... wasn't he? I asked him. 'Yes and no ...' He confessed to me that he had a Sri Lankan wife. He married her many years ago when his parents were very ill. They had arranged the marriage and he wanted to make them happy before they died. True or not? It was quite possible; as a son in Sri Lanka, one would actually do such a thing. The parents are held in the highest esteem and nothing is done to upset them or break with them. His story went on that his wife did not like him because he was fat and she did not like sex, which he loved. So, they separated and lived in the same village for several years now, but just like divorced people. True or not true? I did not know. This uncertainty made life in Sri Lanka a big challenge: as a foreigner you could only live on the information that was given to you. The truth could be quite different. The news with his Sri Lankan wife did not shock me; I felt he was telling the truth about the separation. The story before and where he really lived ... no idea. But, I didn't want anything from him but a little pleasure.

So we met again, which was always difficult to arrange, because Bandula had rare and irregular days off. His employer disposed of him at his whim. If he was bored in the evening because there were no guests, he needed someone to talk to and drink with. Then he called his good friend Bandula, who had to jump. Sometimes he managed to switch off his mobile phone, but after two hours he had a bad conscience and had to check how many missed calls he had and from whom. There was soooo much to share with his friends, in both directions. Bandula had a very best friend, Asanta, to whom he, I think, told about every second he spent with me. They met as often as possible and they talked on the phone several times a day. When I asked what they had to discuss, Bandula said 'We are discussing you, darling.' Oh my goodness, I didn't really like that. I also found out that Bandula was getting calls from friends telling him 'I saw Madam on the bicycle on Galle Road, near Commercial bank.' And later he called me to tell me that I had been seen on Galle Road. Very interesting! Once again, I thought that the concept of privacy is really unknown here. And also: don't they have anything more important to do? So, I was interesting, and I was observed. But now, for reasons that never fully revealed themselves to me, nobody should know that we had a special relationship. It had to remain secret, absolutely! When I suggested we go on a trip, away from this area with its thousand eyes, Bandula was thrilled. The only problem was we had to wait until he finally had a day off. When the day finally came, we drove in his tuktuk to a beach south of Bentota, where a coral reef offers some protection so you can lie in the water and relax. Of course, Bandula couldn't swim and so we couldn't really get out into the sea. I tried again and again to encourage him to practice in my pool. But he didn't really enjoy it and after two minutes he was already exhausted. No stamina at all! By the way, we also had sex in the pool once, which had always been a secret dream of mine. But it is not as easy as you think. Gravity is missing. Turned out to be less dreamy that I had anticipated haha ... Anyway, we enjoyed the day at the beach, bobbed in the shallow water, went to a beach restaurant for dinner and smiled a lot at each other. Bandula was like a big kid and we could also play and laugh together like kids; it did me good. There was not so much to talk about. We came from different worlds and, as I said, we didn't speak the same language. But something about his gentle, bearded company was good for me. He was always extremely affectionate, treated me like his queen and tried to fulfil my every wish. I enjoyed that very much, and my wounded soul slowly relaxed. In spite of my initial intention to limit our relationship to the physical level, after a few weeks, I had developed loving feelings for him. He called me Mannika, his jewel. A pet name that many women in Sri Lanka get, I know. But I felt that I was something special, something valuable for him and I enjoyed it. Bandula helped me to bring my inner light to shine again. Once we drove in his tuktuk and he sent me air kisses through the outside mirror. I sat behind him and my hair, which had been very short when I emigrated, was blowing in the wind. It made me feel much more feminine and soft. Bandula loved my light blonde hair very much. He turned around and said 'Look, your hair is dancing, I love you so much, darling!' And that melted my heart. He was really cute!

After a few weeks I wanted to go on a longer trip with Bandula and we decided to stay one night together in Unawatuna. This is the bay in the very south of the island, where I had spent my birthday and where I now knew some of the nice restaurants and guesthouses. My sweetheart actually got two days off in a row and off we went! As it would have taken about one and a half hours with the tuktuk and it was not very comfortable, we decided to go by bus. We had the choice between two types of buses: there were the cheap public buses, which are always crowded, and with open windows and doors, driving at breakneck speed towards their destination. Some of them even have holes in the floor; they really look as if they will fall apart at any moment. Mostly they are on the wrong lane because they are constantly overtaking. A colourful disco light flickers above the driver, constantly changing colour. Next to it is a picture of Buddha (who may protect us all) and a huge loudspeaker from which the radio blares local hits. The tickets cost little, but these buses are extremely uncomfortable: the benches are so narrow that I, as a northern European, can hardly sit on them and the distance to the front seat is too short for my long legs. But most of the time, there are no free seats at all, and the standing does not increase the driving pleasure. I did not like to take such buses, partly because I was afraid I would not survive the trip. Also, the men took advantage of the tightness to touch my body. This was not only the case with me – it was also common with local women. All reasons enough to prefer an alternative, which is more expensive but much more comfortable. Then there were the so-called AC buses: they are smaller and in better shape. And they are more comfortable in the heat, as the AC stands for Air Condition. They can take a maximum of about thirty passengers with only twenty seats. In the middle of the aisle there are seats that can be folded up or down depending on how full the bus is. So, it is a permanent opening and closing when someone has to get off and needs the middle aisle. But if one has got a seat at the window and drives a longer distance, it is comfortable. The windows and doors stay closed because of the air conditioning and so the exhaust fumes stay outside. The music is a bit less loud and the benches are softer. This costs more, in our case it was two euros per person, but for me it was well affordable. So Bandula and I took such a luxury bus on the way to our love vacation. To keep the whole enterprise as secret as possible, he got on at a different stop than I did. Absolutely ridiculous, I thought, but apparently quite important to him. In Unawatuna, we got off the bus and reached the row of guesthouses by a short walk along the beach road. I had already reserved a room in a nice little house for two nights. Marc, the Australian owner, still knew me from my visit with Angela on my birthday and greeted me joyfully. After a little chat, we honeymooners finally wanted to be alone and went to our room. We both had the urgent need to wash the sweat and street dust off our bodies and Bandula was amazed about the huge bathroom and the beautiful white towels. Marc had recently renovated the rooms and had beautiful furniture brought from Colombo. For my friend it was pure luxury and I too enjoyed the comfort and beauty of our love nest. We had a great time in the big bathtub with lots of bubbles and a lot of laughter and then cuddled up in our king-size bed. Oh, it was nice without neighbours eavesdropping or watching us! I loved to cuddle up to Bandula's soft body and we fooled around for quite a while.

Hunger then drove us out of bed. Ready equipped for the afternoon at the beach, we left our room and went to a beach restaurant. Since Bandula couldn't read the menu in English, I made some suggestions. He immediately decided to have fried rice, a mountain of white rice with some threads of vegetables in it (Sri Lankan style), fried in a pan. Since I had known him for a while now, I realised that he had chosen the cheapest dish for himself. And I knew that he ate fried rice really often and with pleasure. But why again today?! I told him that I wanted him to enjoy it and that I would be happy if he chose something he wouldn't get otherwise. After some wrestling and discussion with the waiter (a long debate, which probably also clarified questions about the home village and the relationship to me), he finally decided to have grilled fish. I chose the same, plus fries. I was a bit fed up with rice by this point, so if I ever had the chance to eat in a restaurant, it had to be potatoes. We enjoyed the moment, our bare feet in the warm sand, the splashing of the waves in our ears and the reggae from the loudspeakers. Perfect holiday mood: yes, that's how Sri Lanka should always be. How different Chamara and Bandula were: Chamara would not have hesitated to order what he wanted. He would have ordered it himself without asking me, and probably three dishes for the two of us - he always exaggerated in everything. But fortunately, this man was far away, and I was happy to have Bandula's company - even in silence. After relaxing a little on the nice loungers in front of the restaurant, we needed to cool down. The beach was different every day; it was formed by the wind and waves of the previous day. On the weekend it was dropping quite steeply towards the water and the water was getting deeper quickly. Bandula got scared just as the sea reached his knees and turned back. Watching me swim was enough for him. I enjoyed being carried by the salty water and was simply happy. So, it was possible to experience love in Sri Lanka after all! I loved the moment! I loved life!

When I realised that I had perhaps developed deeper feelings for Bandula after all, my heart skipped a beat. Jesus, it really didn't have to be like this! In the meantime, we had returned to our everyday life. The two days had been beautiful, and I realized that I was in love with Bandula. My happiness seemed to be written all over my face, because an acquaintance spoke to me: 'You are radiant, are you in love?' There was no reason for me to keep it a secret. So I joyfully told her about Bandula and me. She said, 'You mean the Bandula with the black tuktuk? The Bandula who works at Kingfisher?' 'Yeah, that's the one, all right.' She swallowed and was now quite serious. 'But ... you know he's married?' 'Yes,' I said, 'of course I know that, he told me. But his wife and him don't live together and ...' I explained everything I knew about the relationship. She remained serious. 'No, not that woman.' 'What? There's another one?' 'Yes, he is married to a French woman! She comes here on holiday once a year, and they see each other.' I was serious now, and shocked, and an old wound in me started throbbing terribly. Lying again? Fooled again? You've got to be kidding me! We talked for a while, she told me what she knew, and I felt that she was telling the truth. Why would she lie? For Bandula, on the other hand, there were clear reasons. When I got home, I called him and asked him, 'You have a wife in France?' He was taken by surprise: 'No, no, I can explain! Bandula not lying. Darling don't be angry with me! I tell you later. Now I am busy.' Cut. Conversation over. I've seen this before ... I was thunderstruck. Tears were running and I was deeply, deeply sad. He didn't answer the phone that day. The next was a text message: 'Darling I love you so much. I don't love Marie. She has not come to Sri Lanka for two years. Please don't be angry.' Jesus, what else could I feel but anger! What a country this was! Land like no other is what the tourist ads promise. Yes, that's what it felt like: a country like no other. In my sheltered world, I encountered no liars or cheats before coming to Sri Lanka, and this country seemed to be teeming with them! There was radio silence for a week or two. Then came another message from him 'I love you so much. I want to see you. We must talk.' Okay, I had some things to say. We met that night in a restaurant. I was calm, but clear: our relationship was over. Finished! He started to cry. What a mess! Who was lying, who had the right to cry? He tried to explain to me in stammered sentences what the truth was: that he had actually married Marie. That the authorities in Sri Lanka had not noticed that he was already married to a local woman. I see. That Marie was not as beautiful as me and he no longer loved her. And that she hadn't been there for two years. He wanted a divorce, but it cost so much money. And she didn't want a divorce either. They'd already discussed it on the phone. For whatever reason ... He was now the poor man, trapped in a hopeless situation, sob, if I left him now as well, sob sob sob ... I was the love of his life. It was unbearable. We went round in circles with our words, but there was actually nothing to talk about. And yet we tried, both of us constantly repeating ourselves. 'You lied to me!' 'Bandula not lying!' In this moment,

I realised that we were not only speaking different languages, but we also seemed to live in different realities, seeing the world through different eyes. I got up to leave, and he followed me. Unfortunately, there was no other way for me to get back to my bungalow than with him. No tuktuks for miles. So, I let him drive me. We stopped at my gate and he seriously expected me to invite him in. Which I didn't. In tears, he turned his wedding tuktuk over and rattled away through the silent night. Luckily, I had my dogs. I had to hug them tight.

CHAPTER 31:
Time to Go Back

My time as a teacher was coming to an end. A whole year had passed, and I had to decide how and where I wanted to live on. Actually, I felt a great sense of freedom: I was independent and could make a new beginning anywhere in the world. Only - the choice was almost too big, and I didn't feel like doing something new and strange. My appetite for the exotic was satisfied. I wanted to live in an environment whose rules I knew, and which was well-disposed towards me. And where I could talk in complete sentences. In Sri Lanka, I had gained a small insight into life as a woman traveling alone. The chance was great that I would be lied to and exploited again and again. I did not want to take any risks or experience that sort of trauma again. I did not want to challenge that again. I couldn't imagine a job there that fulfilled me and brought me so much money that I could comfortably live on it. So, I decided to return to Europe. For good. I was ready now. Now I had to choose between Germany and Switzerland. Since I had lived in Switzerland for over twenty years before I emigrated to Sri Lanka and still had some friends there, I was drawn back. I applied again to my old employer and was once again welcomed with open arms. I was a lucky girl, all in all! Before my departure, I still had time to visit some friends. Of course, I went to my angel Angela and we talked a lot, about us, about Sri Lanka, and about life. We did not know if we would meet again. In the meantime, she had married her Sri Lankan boyfriend and was very happy. It was good to see that love exists. I drove once more to the Dolphin Villa and said goodbye to the boys there. Despite the change of ownership, the same employees still worked there with whom I had celebrated my fiftieth birthday, and I was still welcomed like an old friend. 'Very sad you are leaving, Madam. When you come back to Sri Lanka?' Never! I wanted to say. But it only felt right for a part of my heart, the half that was still healing. 'We will see,' replied the half that still had the old longing for this country and its people with the shining eyes.

Once again, I dissolved the possessions that I had accumulated over last year: some small furniture, bed linen, cooking pots, clothes. I gave away everything that I could not take with me to acquaintances and friends. This time the farewell was easy for me, no drama. It felt right. I travelled back to Switzerland and resumed my work for the health insurance company. This time I lived in Winterthur, in a shared flat with a woman of the same age. We had found each other on the internet. The apartment was furnished and offered me perfect conditions for a new start. I was quickly reintegrated, and soon everything ran along familiar lines. This was good, so that I could calm down after the turbulences of the last years. Bandula wrote to me from time to time; I answered in short words, sometimes dismissive. Once he phoned me. I wanted closure and called him back. He cried again: 'Darling I miss you so much,' and I told him once more that I wasn't coming back. That's not to say that I didn't miss him terribly. But my mind triumphed over the remainder of the attachment. Head over heart this time. Where was this going? I too had tears in my eyes when I hung up. There was nothing more to say. It was over. Then I raised my head and looked out through the window of my living room. It had rained, the sky was dark grey. In the last drizzle, two rainbows had formed. Bright and shining, they spanned the sky. They touched my heart and I had to laugh through my tears. A sign from heaven, a confirmation. I had done everything right! I had passed the test at the end. I quickly left my apartment and went out into the drizzle. Barefoot, I walked through the puddles. I felt free and ready to finally put the past behind me. With one big step I jumped through the rainbows, into my new life.

Sri Lanka Calling

CHAPTER 32:

And How Do I Live Now?

Since then, further years have passed and now I am sitting at my desk in Switzerland. It has been ten years since I emigrated to Sri Lanka. I had first returned to Winterthur and after a while I had my own apartment there, my own furniture - finally. But then the sea called so loudly for me that I had to leave again. Since Switzerland has no sea, I chose the German Baltic coast. There I found a job as an assistant doctor in a rehab clinic for psychosomatics near Rostock. Once again, I dissolved my apartment (sold and gave away all my new furniture – how many times has it been now?) and moved back to my native country of Germany, after twenty-eight years abroad. Unfortunately, even this did not last long: the old structures in the clinic, the way of working – it was not for me. I became very ill, coughing all the time, and for weeks I had severe sore throats. My family doctor wrote me off sick; I needed time to make a decision. After only three months, I left the Baltic Sea, totally exhausted, helpless, aimless. I moved to Hamburg, where my parents and sisters live. There, as if by magic, I found an affordable apartment in Eppendorf, which was a real miracle - a schoolmate was able to help me through her connections. The Swiss health insurance company offered me a job again in their home office in Hamburg, which I gratefully accepted. It went well for exactly eighteen months until my work from abroad was no longer allowed. The IT department had a new boss who was concerned about data security and felt it was too risky to allow someone in a different country to do this work. So, I had a choice: I could find another job and stay in Germany, or keep the same job and move back to Switzerland. My goodness! I was not in the mood for another international move at all. I was too tired for another new start. What could I do? Yet I didn't feel like staying in Hamburg at all; I missed the beautiful nature of Switzerland, the crystal-clear lakes. From a distance, I saw the advantages more clearly than when I had lived there. I listened again and again to what my gut was telling me. How should my story continue? So ... yes, I moved again. I found, again by pure magic, a great and affordable apartment very close to beautiful Lake Zurich, from where I could easily commute by the S-Bahn commuter rail to Winterthur to work at the health insurance company. Often, I could work from home and enjoyed the view over the lake, the vastness. Since December 2019, I have been following my inner voice again: I have dared to take the leap into professional independence! After my return to Switzerland, I began hosting workshops and spiritual evenings, alongside working for the health insurance company. Also, while living in Hamburg, I had my business website set up and did coaching sessions part-time. Though the work as a doctor for the medical helpdesk had many advantages, including a regular income, I did not feel happy or fulfilled. My soul was longing for a more holistic work, where I could combine my professional and life experiences to support my clients. It became increasingly draining for me to switch between the different energies of a 'normal' job and my spiritual work. So, I finally listened to my inner voice and took this leap of faith! I am now working full-time as a spiritual seminar leader and give individual coaching on health and life topics. My own life experiences are a valuable basis for this work, and I am happy to inspire other people with my stories.

I think about Sri Lanka a lot. Without melancholy, without anger, without regret. Okay, sometimes with a kind of homesickness. I want to celebrate my sixtieth birthday there in 2021, with Angela. She still lives on the island and has found her niche - even though she is now divorced from her Sri Lankan husband! Sri Lanka is and will always be a part of my life. Without the experiences I had there, I would not be the woman I am now. And whom I like! So, the desire arose to write down my experiences. I felt the need to revisit and organise these important experiences of my life. It touched me very much to observe myself from a safe distance. To feel once again how I went through all those many painful moments. Once again, I felt the loneliness and loss, and also the regret that everything was so difficult. And in those moments, it still hurt a little. But I also felt that my experiences in Sri Lanka weren't all painful. I also got to know honest, dear people. There were many beautiful moments and I am glad that I had the courage to live my dream. Before my emigration, I was not happy. Since the separation from my husband, or even long before that, my heart was closed. I was not really living at all. Behind high walls, I hid from life and from possible further injuries. Chamara managed to blow a hole in this fortress and even finally managed to bring down the walls around my heart. With that, I was open for new experiences. Bandula then filled the resulting emptiness with so much love. And I myself managed to get rid of the last pieces of rubble and learn self-love. I saved myself! Not everyone can do that. I am grateful for these experiences and, honestly, also proud. My life had high waves and I rode them – I did not hide. My head was often under water and I swallowed a lot of sand. But today I feel stronger, more mature, healthier, more fun-loving and more attractive than before I left for Sri Lanka. I am full of ideas for my future and I now create my life very consciously. When I look in the mirror, I see a mature woman of fifty-nine years with a lot of life experience, and I often tell myself how much I like myself. How much I love myself. My friends confirm to me what I myself feel in comparison with old photos: I look twenty years younger than before my time in Sri Lanka. I was old before, now I am young again. I feel great! I am no longer a victim of external circumstances. I live my life, I also take risks, but listen much better to my inner voice. And I can only recommend everyone to live their dreams. Try it! Jump! Have courage! Dreams are an important part of us, a part that wants to live. I've learned to let my gut tell me what I need to know. I will continue to travel, to experience new things, because that is what it means to really live. Not stopping, but always moving. What does the film Finding Nemo say? 'Just keep swimming!' The important thing is that I have found peace. I returned to my kingdom after my travels, like the great Ulysses. My kingdom is not an island in the Mediterranean, it's inside me. The feeling of loneliness has disappeared. I feel connected, welcome, loved. Because I love myself at last. That's what the journey was for. Ulysses, too, matured in his travels. When he came home, his beloved wife and son were waiting for him. It wasn't like that with me. But I am sure there is a partner for me, someone who has been on his own travels and arrived at his own home. I want my partner to have had similar deep experiences or insights about life. I do not search any more. I will stay here for now and live my life. We will find each other!

CHAPTER 33:
From a Distance, Everything Looks Different - What the Stars Say

Even after my return from Sri Lanka I thought a lot about the why. I wanted so much to understand! Why did my heart pull me again and again to Sri Lanka? Why did I have so much bad luck there? And of course: at what point should I have turned back? A good friend who lives in Switzerland knows my whole story. She followed my whole journey from close by and gave me the feeling over all these years that she stood by me. Not everyone was able to do that. She was there for me, without judgement, without shaking her head, a true friend. I had to say goodbye to many friends on my seemingly confused path through life. They just couldn't keep up with my speed and maybe they couldn't understand me either; I cannot say. This faithful friend and I talked about my experiences and the many changes after my return. One day, she had the idea to look at my life under the aspect of the stars. She offered to create my horoscope and then to look for parallels to the horoscope of Sri Lanka as if it was a person. As Sri Lanka's birthday, she chose the date the island achieved its independence, on 4 February 1948. This sounded interesting and I accepted her offer with thanks. And this was the result: as a Gemini, movement plays a big role in my life. It looks as if I will continue to travel, move around, gain experience. This is shown by the horoscope that she created for me alone. But what she then read from the combination of the two horoscopes blew my mind! It took my understanding of what I experienced to another level. Here is her text:

When I look at the horoscopes, at first glance I notice the many similarities between the two, but also many tensions and blockages. I would have been surprised if you hadn't left! For your part, there were many longings then, for the sea, for vastness, for the diversity of nature, the exotic and so on. Maybe old memories from former lives were awakened in your subconscious. I think that you have been there before. Your hunger for experience was great, as were your expectations. You also wanted to turn your back on the pressure to perform, your heart longed for love, you wanted to be free. But there was also a strong spiritual longing there, a search for borderline experiences, for expanding your horizons, for warmth, happiness, comfort, security. And you wanted a partner after your marriage was divorced. You had your western ideas of equal partnership and sharing of resources. But the Sri Lankans have other ideas of marriage, family and partnership. The horoscope of Sri Lanka shows me that. So, there, two worlds collide.

Before you, there stood people from the past, from past lives. You had vague memories. I'm guessing these people used to work for you. Maybe you were a landowner and they were your subjects. You felt the attraction and probably the people in Sri Lanka felt the same. They too had desires, wishes, demands, just like you, but the intentions and positions were very different. They have an old score to settle, you owe them something! And you came to this country and you had much to give: experience, know-how about websites and the internet, you had a good education, the courage for new beginnings and, above all, an open heart. You were ready to give a lot to start a new life. You were ready to share your treasures on many levels with them. Under these conditions, you emigrated to Sri Lanka. It was a gut decision. I see a strong influence of Saturn in the horoscopes. All your visits there have been under its energy, for Saturn in your horoscope falls exactly on the lunar node in the Sri Lankan chart. Saturn stands for destiny in life and the lunar node stands for the gateway of destiny. When these two stars come together, it means that karma is leading you to where circumstances can manifest to redeem (balance) it. So, the people of Sri Lanka claim what you owe them from past lives. You, however, may learn humility.

My friend writes even more and goes into details in some areas of life, which I will skip here. Finally, she says: It was about a transformation in Sri Lanka. You were allowed to balance the old and let go. One could say that parts of you died and new parts could be born. You have managed to reach a higher spiritual level. You have passed an important test! Congratulations!

I was very excited when I read this. From this point of view, everything that happened was meaningful! There really are no coincidences! Yes, I suppose it was the greatest relief to find meaning in all the pain. And I felt validated that it was right to follow my gut feeling. I was meant to go to Sri Lanka and have these experiences exactly as I had them! My path was the logical consequence of influences that were beyond my sight. An infinite relief flowed through me. If I thought I had already made peace with my experiences, then I now felt a new depth, an acceptance. Wow, in the end I had done everything right! But even this feeling could still reach a deeper level. The peace became even more all-encompassing and brought me an unusual compassion for myself and all those involved in my life story. And this came with the colours of Colour Mirrors. I hear you asking, What are 'Colour Mirrors'? Read on...

CHAPTER 34:

Colours Give Me Insights into Past Lives

In 2017, I lived in Hamburg. The first edition of this book was published in 2016 by Amazon, under the pseudonym Carola Wiederkehr, and I only thought of it when I received an email from a reader. In the book, I had given an email address and was delighted when a large number of women used this opportunity to get in contact with me. Besides working for the Swiss health insurance company, I followed my wish to nourish my spiritual side and visited seminars by Diana Cooper, a world-renowned spiritual teacher and bestselling author from England. I then decided to offer such courses myself and completed my training as a teacher on the topic of angels. I then went on to complete teacher training in many different subjects, including unicorns, Lemurian planetary healing, and the Transform Your Life program. In the Diana Cooper School of White Light, an international network of teachers, Diana's knowledge is passed on, and I attended such a course in Southern Germany. Since then, I have hosted angel evenings and taught day courses on angels in Hamburg. My heart was now drawn to a new topic: the magic of Atlantis was calling me. Diana Cooper had written a book about Atlantis which fascinated me, and I felt strongly connected to these energies. There is a teacher for Golden Atlantis in Southern Germany, but I could not imagine hearing the call of the dolphins in this environment. Besides, I love travelling, and so, I went to Spain! I booked a course on Atlantis near Alicante, with the goal to offer seminars on the topic myself afterwards. I could not have guessed that there, of all places, I would get further insights into my experiences in Sri Lanka. But so it was!

My teacher's name was Penny Wing, and the class was in English. And I was the only student in those six days. I learned a lot about the way of life of the Atlanteans, the high priests of the time, the twelve chakras and their angels, numerology, crystals, and much more. Dolphins also played a role in Atlantis, of course; it is said that they still carry the knowledge of the lost continent within them. There was a lot to learn, but there was also a lot of time in the private lessons to dive into my own topics. Spiritual courses are not only about absorbing knowledge but also about one's own healing. Since I was alone, we were able to give space to what was coming up.

Penny liked to supplement her courses with the use of the Colour Mirrors Bottles. These are bottles similar to those of Aurasoma. The clear glass bottles have a flattened round body and contain two coloured liquids that do not mix because one is oily and the other is aqueous. These bottles carry a certain energy, and the founder of Colour Mirrors, Melissie Jolly, gives channelled information to each bottle, which can be used in healing work. For example, one can ask: What should Kerstin learn in Sri Lanka? Which energy from past lives led to the experiences in Sri Lanka? And then you intuitively look for a colour combination that appeals to you or a number that leads you to a bottle.

At some point in the Atlantis class we talked about numerology. The Atlanteans knew the meaning of numbers and used it. They knew that our birthday carries an important energy and tells us something about our mission in life. The priests could then pass this knowledge on to those seeking advice and help them to make important decisions in their lives. The birthday reflects our task, just like our name, whose letters can also be looked at numerologically. In this course, we looked at my birthday from this point of view and found the number 28 (or 1 if you reduce it further). The bottle with the number 28 contains a bright yellow above a light turquoise. The message of this bottle is: New beginnings.

New Beginnings (Yellow over Pale Turquoise)

More than any other, this bottle is about a new beginning. These colours indicate that the door is finally opening in a very real and accessible way to a new era of happiness and sunshine. This bottle relates to the goddess Lakshmi, who brings good fortune in her wake and whose message is to love your life. You cannot fight or panic it into being better, you can only love it into joy. These colours bring trust, laughter and a sense of fun, and as there is nothing that will bring about a new beginning faster than joy, this bottle will help you create the reality that serves you best. Stop worrying – everything is going to be fine.

So, in connection with my birthday, this meant that I could have confidence that everything was good. That I had support from Lakshmi and that I could bring more joy into my life. The colours yellow and turquoise could help me in this. Penny, as an experienced interpreter of Colour Mirrors, saw even more in this bottle: she was sure that I had lived in Atlantis and that I carried its energies within me. Now was the time to live these energies again, to bring them out and create a new Golden Age, together with all other people. So, I was a perfect teacher to pass on the knowledge of Atlantis. This touched a string in me that resonated. Yes, I could imagine feeling that I had lived in Atlantis. And I really do give seminars with my heart's blood to connect more people with these energies. That was the first part of the message the magic bottles of Colour Mirrors had for me.

We then asked about the relationship with my ex in Sri Lanka. I intuitively chose one number for him and one for me, and Penny put the bottles with the two numbers on the table. The message that came out of this combination then blew my mind: they were saying that I had lived in Egypt in another life! I had been a rich person, probably a man of influence and possession. Slaves were a part of it as well. Chamara's bottle showed that he had a relationship with Nubia. So, it is possible that in the life I was incarnated in Egypt, he was there as well, as a slave on my estate. That completely knocked me out! I immediately felt a deep resonance to this picture, to the idea that Chamara had to work for me in a past life for years, maybe his whole life, without pay. And because of my understanding of karma, it is clear that at some point a compensation must be made - as it happened in Sri Lanka. He took what was due to him and now we were even! Wow, that made sense! The sad thing was that he had none of the money left. He was still poor, because he used the money to repay old debts. In this way, he rebalanced his own karma. At some point, the balance is achieved, then we are really free. From this point of view, I had taken an important and right step on my soul's path! A further validation, which I greatly appreciated.

The whole subject of karmic compensation fascinates me very much. I am a human being and I think logically; I want to understand - and the law of karma is logical. I studied for many years in a Buddhist centre in Lucerne and we worked very intensively on it. At that time, we compared karma to a spiritual bank, where you can have credit but also debts. But, at some point, the account has to be balanced and our soul is looking for ways to do this. At that time, I understood this theoretically, but only today, with the help of current examples, I feel that it is our reality, that all our lives are determined by it. When Diana Cooper writes that by 2032 we may already have a New Golden Age, doubts always come up. Don't we have an enormous amount of dark, heavy, difficult things happening on Earth at the moment? The news keeps us up to date on earthquakes, bush fires, hurricanes, wars, pandemics, and much more, spread across the planet. It is possible that all of this has to do with the balancing of karma. That many things that had been swept under the carpet, many debts, so to speak, are now being balanced. And that will cause upheaval, pain, grief, loss. It is a purification of every single person and our planet. When I look at it that way, I can cope better with all the disasters. Then there is a purpose behind it. Then in the end everything is perfect - as it is now. As in every moment. Because everything is part of life. And life is good!

Sri Lanka Calling

CHAPTER 35:

My Outer Journey was an Inner Journey

After my findings through the Colour Mirrors Bottles in the Atlantis course, it was not surprising that I wanted to learn more about them. These bottles really seem to be able to speak! So, I attended an intensive course on this topic in 2018 and was able to travel to sunny Spain again. Penny was again the perfect teacher for me, and she accompanied me with a lot of empathy and intuition. I learned that my family name, Joost, numerologically breaks down to the number seven. Which confirmed that I am a spiritual teacher. That this was my purpose in life. The number one (the sum of the numbers two and eight from the sum of my birth date, twenty-eight) says that my spiritual ascension is an important issue in this life. We then looked at various aspects in the context of numerology, which result from my name and birthday. I was deeply moved by Penny's statement that writing was an important part of me. That my deep feelings wanted to be expressed through writing. And - now I have goose bumps - that

I should share my experiences on my spiritual path with others. This was an important part of my life's work! So, without this information, I had already intuitively done the right thing when I wrote this book. I had listened to my gut feeling and done the right thing. Again! There were many reasons not to publish this book (and I published it under a pseudonym in the beginning), but shame was the strongest of all. But I did it anyway – it just felt right! The writing and the whole processing afterwards helped me a lot and I realised that I can inspire other people. I want to say that I would never force my opinion on others. I would not say: Well, be happy, you have balanced your account in the karma bank! Everybody has the possibility to see their experience as they choose to see it. Betrayal, robbery, cheating. That's how we experience it in our world. But on a deeper level, it was the result of our actions in previous lives or earlier in this life. And for me, it is helpful to understand my story on this level. I never wrote anything similar in the online forums for women who had gone through similar experiences to mine, where I was active for a short time, because it was a protected space for injured souls, which I did not want to disturb. But if someone asks me, if someone is looking for healing, for understanding, I offer my experiences. Everyone has the right to their own view. I can only say that, through my experiences, I have gone through a deep healing. That the spiritual view of the experience has brought me further, has helped me. That after the valley of tears I am definitely on the mountain of joy and have found new confidence in myself and the whole process of life. I realised that the decision to go to Sri Lanka and everything connected with it was just as it should be. That every step, every move in my life had a meaning and led me exactly where I was supposed to be. Even if it looked very chaotic and restless to human eyes - and it felt that way at times. I always followed my inner guidance, which had the big picture in mind. I can trust my gut feeling again; in truth, it has never deceived me. And that is a very important insight! I wish so much to inspire many people with my story!

In summary, I have learned a lot from my experiences. I have printed out these reminders and hung them above my desk:

- Follow your gut. Your gut carries your wisdom from this life and also from past lives. Trust it.
- Connect with your companions in the spiritual world, the angels, unicorns, fairies, dragons, Ascended Masters. Ask them for guidance and protection. They see your life from a higher perspective and help you to make decisions for your highest good.
- Seek support, comfort, courage, therapy with good friends, therapists or spiritual teachers as needed. You do not have to travel this path alone!
- Live your feelings! Feel the pain, the helplessness, the anger or disappointment. Express them through movements, sounds, artistic channels. Then, move on; don't get stuck in them. Avoid self-pity: it's a dead end.
- Forgive those who hurt you! Forgive yourself! It's essential. You don't need to approve of what happened. But you can take away its power over yourself and find inner peace.
- Have compassion for everyone you meet, and for yourself. Earth seems to be a planet full of challenges. But it is also the planet with the greatest potential for your soul to learn. And that's exactly why you are here.

- Love yourself with all your heart! Learn to love yourself first, then share that love with others.
- Remember that you only see and experience a small part of the story. The reasons for this can be found in past lives. It makes sense that you are now experiencing exactly what is happening. Have faith in the divine plan. You yourself have determined before you were born what you want to learn in this life. Now accept this task completely, and also trust in yourself that you can do it.
- Know this: there are no such things as mistakes! All choices are steps on the way to learn something. A child who learns to walk does not make any mistakes; they make progress with every attempt. Find positive words and feelings for yourself and avoid negative ones.
- Don't condemn yourself or anyone else. We are all part of a big whole and we all play a role. We are all here to gain experience and grow. Someone has to take on the role of the oppressor so that you can learn to forgive and love unconditionally. Look at life as a play on a stage, and sometimes step into the role of the spectator. This creates distance to the drama that is happening on stage right now.
- You're perfect just the way you are!! Always remember that, and believe it! Because it's true. You are perfect.

CHAPTER 36:

My Offerings

Those notes above my desk always remind me of my discoveries, as if they were treasures inside me. All too quickly, I could forget them in my everyday life. I know that many other people feel the same way I do. That is why these beliefs can be found in all my seminars in one form or another. Be it in connection with angels, with Atlantis, heart opening, forgiveness, chakra work, and so on. Maybe you will discover your own interest in one of these topics. At the moment, I live near Zurich, in Switzerland, where I also offer events. But right now, I am working on offering courses online in the form of webinars, which you can attend from all over the world. Because for me, a clear vision for my next steps in life has emerged from the depth of my heart: I will move again. Travelling will continue to have a great significance in my life. But I have found my home, and it is within me, in my inner peace. That is true home. The surroundings are secondary. But to keep my creativity flowing, I will spend more time by the sea. The Mediterranean soothes me. I want to write spiritual books there to inspire people. And I will help people through online courses to connect with their soul - and with the helpers in the spiritual world. Because we are really never alone on our travels. I am convinced of that!

I am also using my own experiences to help others through the process of overcoming emotional trauma and stepping into their power, enabling them to move forward with their lives. For information about my online workshops and coaching programs, please feel free to reach out and email me at kontakt@kerstinjoost.com. I am always happy to hear from my readers. On my website, www.kerstinjoost.com, you will find information about my current seminars as well as details about my coaching. I hope to hear from you soon!

In closing, I would like to share an excerpt from The Archangel Guide to Enlightenment and Mastery by Diana Cooper and Tim Whild, which I feel perfectly sums up how I have come to view all of my experiences:

'Some lightworkers talk of amazing journeys of the heart that they have taken without any thought or logic. They step onto a boat or plane to visit a faraway land or sacred site that is calling to them. Or they feel a great desire to live in a certain country and they find themselves there. When this happens to you, your Earth Star is working at its most powerful level. When you reach the chosen site, this chakra will download specific light codes into the planet to activate it at a higher frequency. These journeys will continue to be a vital part of the establishment of the Golden Age here on Earth. Many masters who are pulled to a certain place have already spent powerful lifetimes there. They are returning to finish work that was planned many lifetimes ago'.

Dr Kerstin Joost

I wish you joy on all of your journeys.
With light and love, Dr Kerstin Joost

www.ingramcontent.com/pod-product-compliance
Lightning Source LLC
Chambersburg PA
CBHW071609080526
44588CB00010B/1074